Personal Excellence

Robert K. Throop and
Marion B. Castellucci

ADAPTED BY LEO SEVIGNY

DELMAR
CENGAGE Learning

Australia • Brazil • Japan • Korea • Mexico • Singapore • Spain • United Kingdom • United States

DELMAR CENGAGE Learning

Personal Excellence
Robert K. Throop,
Marion B. Castellucci

Vice President, Career
Education Strategic
Business Unit: Dawn
Gerrain

Director of Editorial: Sherry
Gomoll

Acquisitions Editor:
Martine Edwards

Developmental Editor:
Gerald O'Malley

Editorial Assistant: Jennifer
Anderson

Director of Production:
Wendy A. Troeger

Production Manager:
J. P. Henkel

Production Editor: Nina
Tucciarelli

Director of Marketing:
Wendy E. Mapstone

Channel Manager: Gerard
McAvey

For product information and
technology assistance, contact us at **Cengage Learning
Customer & Sales Support, 1-800-354-9706**

For permission to use material from this text or product,
submit all requests online at **www.cengage.com/permissions**
Further permissions questions can be emailed to
permissionrequest@cengage.com

Library of Congress Control Number: 2005009370

ISBN-13: 978-1-4018-8200-6

ISBN-10: 1-4018-8200-5

Delmar
Executive Woods
5 Maxwell Drive
Clifton Park, NY 12065
USA

Cengage Learning is a leading provider of customized learning solutions with office locations around the globe, including Singapore, the United Kingdom, Australia, Mexico, Brazil, and Japan. Locate your local office at **www.cengage.com/global**

Cengage Learning products are represented in Canada by Nelson Education, Ltd.

To learn more about Delmar, visit **www.cengage.com/delmar**

Purchase any of our products at your local bookstore or at our preferred online store **www.ichapters.com**

Notice to the Reader
Publisher does not warrant or guarantee any of the products described herein or perform any independent analysis in connection with any of the product information contained herein. Publisher does not assume, and expressly disclaims, any obligation to obtain and include information other than that provided to it by the manufacturer. The reader is expressly warned to consider and adopt all safety precautions that might be indicated by the activities described herein and to avoid all potential hazards. By following the instructions contained herein, the reader willingly assumes all risks in connection with such instructions. The publisher makes no representations or warranties of any kind, including but not limited to, the warranties of fitness for particular purpose or merchantability, nor are any such representations implied with respect to the material set forth herein, and the publisher takes no responsibility with respect to such material. The publisher shall not be liable for any special, consequential, or exemplary damages resulting, in whole or part, from the readers' use of, or reliance upon, this material.

Printed in the United States of America
7 8 9 10 11   17 16 15 14 13

This is for my father, Ken, who lives within me;
for my mother, Joie, who always made me feel unique;
for my wife, Joyce, who provides me with unconditional love;
and for my daughters, Tracey, Wendee, and Bethany,
who fill me with resounding joy.
—Robert K. Throop

For my mother, Agatha Eken Bonney.
—Marion B. Castellucci

Contents at a Glance

Contents

>>

Chapter 5 Communicating Effectively   83

Self-belief is the foundation of success in all personal, educational, and professional endeavors. In order to succeed, you must deal with personal, economic, and societal problems and make a commitment to work to achieve your goals. A solid sense of who you are and who you might become is the springboard to overcoming obstacles and succeeding in all areas of life.

Personal Excellence is designed to help you take control of your life and improve your self-belief. This book blends concepts and applications that will help you discover your emotional, intellectual, physical, and social potential. Through a process of learning and self-examination, you will discover your values, increase your commitment to personal goals, and challenge yourself to grow and learn. While gaining practical knowledge and skills, you will discover your emotional, intellectual, physical, and social resources. You will learn that you can improve your life by changing the way you think about yourself—and then acting accordingly.

In the pages of this book you will have an opportunity to engage in several types of exercises and activities, geared toward self-understanding and growth. Because people learn best from their own experiences, *Personal Excellence* offers a unique format that involves you in an active learning process.

ROBERT K. THROOP is the former Corporate Director of Education for ATE Enterprises. With over 35 years of experience in education, spanning the elementary to graduate school levels, he is presently the Chief Academic Officer for ITT Educational Services Inc.

MARION B. CASTELLUCCI earned a B.A. from Barnard College. She has over 25 years' experience as a writer and editor of educational publishing.

Introduction

>>

Whether you are searching for your ideal job or are satisfied with the position you have, today's rapidly changing workplace requires constant personal and professional development. Savvy employees and job seekers understand the need to be prepared for inevitable changes in corporate structure, new job opportunities, and personal lifestyle. The *Pathway to Excellence* series is for anyone looking to build a foundation of effective communication skills, job search techniques, and a personal success plan for growth and promotion in any industry.

The series delivers real-life skills and strategies that can be applied immediately to your personal or professional life. *Personal Excellence* provides a comprehensive guide for success when read cover to cover. The straightforward approach of the text also makes it an excellent reference if you have limited time and need specific advice by topic.

Icons used throughout the book help to highlight key points and exercises.

 Exercises for you to complete

 A helpful perspective on how to accomplish the goal at hand

 A list of common mistakes to be on the lookout for

 A summary of the main points of each chapter

However you make use of the insights in this series, our hope is that you continue to pursue your individual path to excellence.

Chapter 1

The Power of Self-Belief

After Erik Weihenmayer climbed Mt. Everest, he was hailed as the first blind person to reach the top of the world's tallest peak. His achievement was featured in newspapers and magazines and on TV. Weihenmayer was personally congratulated by President Bush in the Oval Office. Weihenmayer's success in climbing Mt. Everest was not an overnight accomplishment. Blinded at age 13, Erik began climbing when he was 16, using his hands and feet to find places to hold on to the rock. Over the

> Success doesn't come to you . . . you go to it.
>
> MARVA COLLINS, AMERICAN EDUCATOR

years, he climbed several of the world's highest mountains, in North America, South America, and Antarctica. Still, climbing Mt. Everest was a lifelong goal. During the Everest climb, Weihenmayer kept reminding himself to stay focused and not let fear and frustration stand in his way. The hardest part of the climb was crossing the Khumbu Icefall. The icefall is 2,000 feet of broken blocks of ice and crevasses so treacherous that climbers can fall to their deaths. Weihenmayer made his way very slowly. He followed directions from the climber ahead of him, who wore a bell on his jacket as a guide.

©DIDRIK JOHNCK/CORBIS

Success requires self-knowledge, motivation, and hard work. Erik Weihenmayer climbed many mountains before tackling Mt. Everest.

Weihenmayer doesn't climb mountains to prove that blind people can do amazing things. To him, that's a side benefit of climbing. Rather, he climbs because he loves it. "It's a lot of hard work," says Weihenmayer, "but there are some really beautiful moments."

What Is Success?

Let's take a moment to think about success. In the United States, success is often equated with glamor, fame, and riches. Or it is thought of as a single achievement—winning an election or getting a good job. Yet leading a successful life is an ongoing process. This chapter will tap into your personal values and beliefs, and give you insight as to how you can bring these personal qualities into focus so that you can achieve the success you desire.

A great example of bringing these qualities together to create success is Jimmy Carter, who was president of the United States, surely one of the peaks of success. But when he returned to Georgia after his presidency, he explored new tasks. Carter's work with Habitat for Humanity, a volunteer organization that helps build and renovate low-income housing, helped that organization grow. He represented the United States on a number of diplomatic missions over the years. In 2002 Carter was awarded the Nobel Prize for Peace primarily for his work after he was U.S. president.

> If we did all the things we are capable of doing, we would literally astonish ourselves.
>
> THOMAS A. EDISON, INVENTOR

Fame and awards are not the only marks of a successful life. A self-perception of worth and good relationships with others are often the basis of a successful life. As golf champion Chi Chi Rodriguez said, "The most successful human being I know was my dad and he never had anything financially."

So people who are truly successful are always trying to fulfill their potential. They focus on possibilities and work to turn them into realities. Furthermore, they see their potential as wide-ranging, from emotional to intellectual, from social to physical. They also see that their potential continues to change and grow as they gain experience. People who are trying to reach their potential know that the pursuit of success is a lifelong process.

Who Are You?

Purpose: Successful people usually have a clear sense of who they are and what they want from life. This exercise will help you to define qualities that you have that define who you are. Take a few minutes to think about yourself and your life. Then answer these questions.

I like:

1._____

2._____

3._____

I appreciate:

1._____

2._____

3._____

I am good at:

1._____

2._____

3._____

Someday I would like to:

1._____

2._____

3._____

Values

People who lead successful lives live by certain values. Values are your deepest feelings and thoughts about yourself and life. Values have three parts: (1) what you think, (2) how you feel, and (3) how you act, based on what you think and feel. For example, one of your values might be honesty. You think that telling a lie is wrong (thought). If someone you trust lies to you, you feel betrayed (feeling). When you make a mistake, you admit it rather than try to cover up or blame someone else (action).

Sometimes the three aspects of values do not always work in harmony. Let's take the value of honesty again. Even though you think telling a lie is wrong, there are times when you think or act as though lying is okay. If someone asks you to do something you don't want to do, you might lie and say you're busy. Lying makes you feel uncomfortable because your actions and thoughts contradict one another. People are most comfortable in situations in which the thinking, feeling, and acting aspects of their values are working together.

Our Society's Values

Although Americans come from many national, ethnic, and racial groups, we share many values. Polls have shown that adult Americans value honesty, ambition, responsibility, and broad-mindedness. We value peace, family security, and freedom. We may not always behave according to our values, but they are the standard against which we judge ourselves. Rank your values in the exercise that follows.

What Do You Value?

Purpose: This exercise will bring into focus what values are most vital to you. Knowing these values will help you understand how your internal drive for success is defined. Following is a list of 15 values arranged in alphabetical order. Study the list carefully. Then place a 1 next to the value most important to you, a 2 next to the value that is second in importance, and so on. The value that is least important to you should be ranked 15.

When you have completed ranking the values, check your list. Feel free to make changes. Take all the time you need so that the end result truly reflects your values.

Value	Rank
Affectionate	_____
Ambitious	_____
Brave	_____
Cheerful	_____
Competent (capable)	_____
Courteous (well-mannered)	_____
Forgiving	_____
Helpful (working for others' welfare)	_____
Honest	_____
Logical	_____
Neat	_____
Obedient (dutiful, respectful)	_____
Open-minded	_____
Responsible	_____
Self-controlled (committed)	_____

A five-year study to determine what 120 of the nation's top artists, athletes, and scholars had in common came up with surprising results. Researcher Benjamin Bloom, professor of education at the University of Chicago, said, "We expected to find tales of great natural gifts. We didn't find that at all. Their mothers often said it was their other child who had the greater gift." The study concluded that the key element common to these successful people was not talent but commitment.

> The only place that success comes before work is in the dictionary.
>
> VIDAL SASSOON,
> SALON PROFESSIONAL

Examine Your Values

Purpose: Now that you have determined some self-important values, it is time to analyze their importance. Answer the following questions about the 15 values you ranked.

1. Why is your top-ranked value so important to you?

_____

_____

_____

2. Describe a situation in which your top-ranked value influenced your behavior.

_____

_____

_____

3. Are there types of situations in your life where some of your top values apply more than others (work, personal life, spiritual life, etc?)

_____

_____

_____

Changing Values

Our values can change as a result of experience. For example, after the terrorist attacks on the United States on September 11, 2001, a shift took place in Americans' values. According to a CBS News/*New York Times* poll taken a year later, 14 percent of Americans reevaluated their lives as a result of the attack. Although many felt the country had not changed, 17 percent thought that communities had become stronger, and 7 percent felt that Americans were more patriotic, had more pride in their country, and were nicer to one another than they had been before.

News & Views

Benjamin Franklin's Values

Throughout history, people have been concerned about figuring out their values and trying to live by them. Benjamin Franklin, the 18th-century American printer, author, diplomat, and scientist, was one of the writers of the

Declaration of Independence. He also helped draft the U.S. Constitution. In his autobiography, Franklin explains how he tried to change his behavior by describing and then trying to live by his values, which he called "virtues." How many of Franklin's values are still important today? Which of Franklin's values do you share?

THE THIRTEEN VIRTUES

1. Temperance: Eat not to dullness. Drink not to elevation.
2. Silence: Speak not but what may benefit others or yourself. Avoid trifling conversation.
3. Order: Let all your things have their places. Let each part of your business have its time.
4. Resolution: Resolve to perform what you ought. Perform without fail what you resolve.
5. Frugality: Make no expense but to do good to others or yourself, i.e., waste nothing.
6. Industry: Lose no time. Be always employed in something useful. Cut off all unnecessary actions.
7. Sincerity: Use no hurtful deceit. Think innocently and justly; if you speak, speak accordingly.
8. Justice: Wrong none by doing injuries or omitting the benefits that are your duty.
9. Moderation: Avoid extremes. Forbear resenting injuries so much as you think they deserve.
10. Cleanliness: Tolerate no uncleanliness in body, clothes, or habitation.
11. Tranquility: Be not disturbed at trifles or at accidents common or unavoidable.
12. Chastity: Rarely use venery* but for health or offspring—never to dullness, weakness, or the injury of your own or another's peace or reputation.
13. Humility: Imitate Jesus and Socrates.†

Source: Franklin, Benjamin, *The Autobiography of Benjamin Franklin and Selections from His Other Writings.* New York: Random House, 1994, pp. 93–95.

*Sexual activity.

†Ancient Greek philosopher who taught about virtue and justice.

Values can also change because of personal experience. A young woman overcame a drug abuse problem with the help of her church's music director. As a result, she became aware of the importance of helping others. Today she is studying to become a psychotherapist so she can help others.

Beliefs

While values are your most deeply held general thoughts and feelings, beliefs are the specific opinions you have about yourself and particular people, situations, things, or ideas. In other words, beliefs are the specific attitudes that arise from your values. For example, if one of your values is ambition, you may have the belief that further education is important for success. If you value helpfulness, you may believe that you should do volunteer work in your community.

The Effects of Beliefs

Psychologists have shown that beliefs have a tremendous influence on behavior, and in turn, behavior can affect beliefs. Aesop's fable about the fox and the grapes shows how this can happen. When the fox first sees the grapes, he thinks they look delicious. This belief influences his behavior. He leaps up again and again, trying to reach the grapes. But the bunch of grapes is too high for him, and he gives up. Frustrated, the fox changes his belief: He decides the grapes must be sour.

This type of interplay between beliefs and behavior goes on all the time. Most of the time, you may not even be aware that it is happening. Yet your beliefs and other people's beliefs about you—both positive and negative—have a powerful influence on how you behave.

Negative Beliefs

Each person has the potential to live a successful and happy life. Yet most of us fall short of that ideal because we are carrying a bag of mental "garbage" that weighs us down. This garbage is negative beliefs about ourselves. Some examples of negative beliefs are

> I can't do algebra.
> I'm not smart enough to do that.
> Nobody cares about me.
> I'll never find a job.

> They cannot take away our self-respect if we do not give it to them.
>
> GANDHI, INDIAN POLITICAL AND SPIRITUAL LEADER

Unfortunately, negative beliefs like these influence our behavior. The person who says she can't learn algebra in fact can't. The person who says he can't find a job doesn't find a job. Why? Because they don't try very hard. They think they will fail and so they do fail. A belief that comes true because it is believed is called a self-fulfilling prophecy.

Positive Beliefs

Self-fulfilling prophecies need not be negative, however. Sometimes they are positive; they enable you to take action and make progress. Some positive, or enabling, beliefs are

> I will find the money to go to school.
> I will speak up even though I'm nervous.
> I'm going to start my own business in five years.
> I will learn to swim.

The power of enabling beliefs is that they often come true. They come true not because of wishful thinking, however. Rather, enabling beliefs help you focus on what you need to do to accomplish something. They give you the self-confidence to persist and succeed.

Others Affect Your Beliefs

Your beliefs about yourself, both positive and negative, are influenced by the people around you. Family, friends, coworkers, and acquaintances all affect your beliefs. For example, many studies have shown the effect of teachers' beliefs on students' performance. In one experiment, 60 preschoolers were taught symbols. One group was taught by instructors who were told to expect good symbol learning. The other group was taught by instructors told to expect poor learning. The results? Nearly 77 percent of the first group of children learned five or more symbols. Only 13 percent of the second group of children learned five or more symbols.

Victims and Nonvictims

If you allow yourself to be persuaded by negative beliefs, you will soon view yourself as a victim. Victims operate from a position of weakness. They think that they are not smart enough or strong enough to take charge of their own lives. They live from day to day, allowing things to happen to them and others to control them.

Nonvictims, on the other hand, understand that negative beliefs can be crippling. Nonvictims have the ability to resist the negative beliefs of others because they believe in their own strengths. Because they have positive views of their abilities and goals, nonvictims often succeed where victims fail. Reverend Jesse Jackson, for example, grew up in poverty and went on to become a political leader and Democratic presidential candidate. "My mother was a teenaged mother and her mother was a teenaged mother. With scholarships and other help, I managed to get an education. Success to me is being born in a poor or disadvantaged family and making something of yourself."

Changing Your Beliefs

We all suffer the effects of negative beliefs, some of us more than others. Sometimes events don't happen the way we expect. Or we fall into a pattern of negative behavior toward the people around us. Or a stressful event or change in our lives throws us off balance. When these situations happen, it's time to pay attention to your beliefs. If your beliefs are contributing to your difficulties, you can change them—and change your life for the better.

Why should you drop negative beliefs and adopt beliefs that will enable you to succeed? Because it works. You must

> understand the power that beliefs have in your life.
> realize that continuing to think in a negative way will harm the quality of your life.
> change your beliefs and how you think about yourself.

If you change your beliefs, you will change your behavior. If you change your behavior, you will change your life.

Linda Pauwels

You may have seen her on CNN, Fox, or Tele-mundo—Captain Linda Pauwels, the only female spokesperson for the Allied Pilots Association. In 2000, at the age of 37, Captain Pauwels became the first Hispanic woman to captain a jet for American Airlines. She has another "first" to her credit. According to the International Society of Women Airline Pilots, Pauwels became the world's youngest female jet captain at age 25.

Nothing in Pauwels's childhood hinted at her future success in aviation. When she was 6, she came to Miami from Argentina with her mother and younger brother. Her mother worked two jobs, and when she could not care for the children, she sent them back to Argentina to stay with family. Pauwels and her brother went back and forth between Miami and Argentina as they grew up.

At age 16, Pauwels returned to the United States for good and earned her GED. She took a job at an aviation company and fell in love with flying. At 17, she earned her private pilot's license. Soon she was test-flying small planes. When she was 22, she went to work for Southern Air Transport—the first female pilot they ever hired.

Today Pauwels wants to establish a foundation to help young Hispanics become pilots. "I want to identify . . . children of character, competent, who you can see are going to make it," explains Pauwels. "I always had people help me." She's also gone back to school for a bachelor of science degree in aeronautics.

Source: Julia Bencomo Lobaco, "Capt. Linda Pauwels: Flying Sky High," *Hispanic,* June 2002, pp. 20, 32; "Pauwels Named Hispanic Business 100 Most Influential Hispanics," *APA Pilot Perspective,* Oct. 14, 2002, p. 2; "Other Notable Firsts," International Society of Women Airline Pilots Web site, http://www.iswap.org/firsts/other.html, accessed January 21, 2003.

Using Positive Self-Talk

That negative inner voice that tells you how bad things are and how bad they always will be has to be silenced. Talking back to that negative voice can help you change your beliefs, attitudes, and behavior.

To change your beliefs and behavior, you needn't talk out loud in public, but you can use positive self-talk. Positive self-talk has three characteristics:

1. Positive self-talk consists of I statements. I statements show that you are taking charge of your life.
2. Positive self-talk uses the present tense. Using the present tense shows you are ready for action.
3. Positive self-talk is positive and enthusiastic. It focuses on what is rather than what is not.

Use Positive Self-Talk

Purpose: Now that you have a strong understanding of the negative impact of self-defeating thoughts, it is important to know how to change your thinking. Each of the following is a negative belief. Rewrite each so that it is positive self-talk.

I'll never get the promotion I want. I come in late too often.

_____

_____

_____

That computer is too hard to operate.

_____

_____

_____

I'll be _____ years old before I get my diploma (or degree or certificate).

_____

_____

_____

Answer the following questions:

Describe a situation about which you had negative thoughts and feelings.

_____

_____

_____

How could you have used positive self-talk to change your beliefs and behavior?

_____

_____

_____

The Seven Beliefs of Successful People

Positive beliefs will empower you to use all your emotional, intellectual, physical, and social potential to make things happen your way. People who consistently succeed can commit all their resources to achieving their goals. Let's examine seven beliefs that many successful people live by.

1. Everything happens for a reason and a purpose. People have both good and bad experiences. Instead of dwelling on the bad, successful people think in terms of future possibilities.

2. There is no such thing as failure. Rather, there are only results. If the result is not desirable, successful people change their actions and produce new results.

3. Whatever happens, take responsibility. Successful people don't blame others when something goes wrong. Taking responsibility is one of the best measures of a person's maturity.

4. It's not necessary to understand everything in order to use everything. Successful people don't get bogged down in every detail. They learn what they need to know and don't dwell on the rest.

5. After yourself, people are your greatest resource. Successful people have a tremendous respect and appreciation for other people. They understand that good relationships are one of the foundations of a successful life.

6. Work is play. No one succeeds by doing something they hate to do. Work should be exciting, challenging, interesting. It should be fun.

7. There's no lasting success without commitment. Successful people are persistent. They keep doing their best.

Self-Belief

The net effect of your values and beliefs is your self-belief. Self-belief is your confidence in and respect for your own abilities. Self-belief is the part of us that is resilient in the face of difficulties. Bad things may happen and hurt us—physically, emotionally, or economically—but our positive self-belief does not need to be harmed. People with positive self-belief understand that outward circumstances do not change this inner belief.

> If you want a quality, act as if you already had it.
>
> WILLIAM JAMES, PSYCHOLOGIST AND PHILOSOPHER

Improving Your Self-Belief

Have you decided that your self-belief is not all it could be? There are ways to improve your self-belief.

> *Accept yourself.* Recognize your own good qualities and don't expect to be perfect. Everyone has special talents and abilities. Work to discover and develop yours.

> *Pay attention to yourself.* Try to discover what gives you inner satisfaction, and do things that give you pleasure. Successful people do what they enjoy.

> *Use positive self-talk.* Encourage yourself to make the most of your abilities by developing a positive mental attitude. People who succeed tell themselves that they will succeed.

> *Don't be afraid to try new things.* Remember that there is no such thing as failure—only results. If you don't try new things, you won't reach your potential.

> *Remember that you are special.* No one else has your set of capabilities and talents. Your values, beliefs, and emotions, and the way you act on them, make up your unique personality.

The Foundation of Success

Positive self-belief is the foundation of success. When you believe in yourself, you can accomplish what you set your mind to. Self-belief allows you to use your emotional, intellectual, social, and physical potential to take action. Taking action means making progress toward achieving your dreams and goals. When you act, you get results. When you get results, your self-belief improves because you've succeeded at something. Improved self-belief gives you the confidence to take further action. The process of building self-belief is cyclical. The more you try, the more you accomplish and the greater your self-belief. Self-belief with commitment can create miracles.

> If you want to succeed in life . . . you . . . need to know what you believe in. . . . Then you have to have the courage to act on those beliefs.
>
> RUDOLPH GIULIANI,
> FORMER MAYOR OF
> NEW YORK CITY

Take the example of Mahatma Gandhi, a man with many exceptional traits, one of which was a strong belief in himself and his abilities. While the Indian power elites were trying to break England's colonial rule with speeches and infighting, Gandhi was out in the countryside working alone with the poor. Gradually he gathered overwhelming support and trust from the ordinary people of India. With no political office or military capability, he and his followers eventually defeated England. India won its independence as a nation.

Although Gandhi was clearly an exceptional person, successful people share some of his characteristics. They are willing to do whatever it takes to reach their potential without harming others. They are not necessarily the "best" or the "brightest," but they have positive self-belief and a strong commitment to their goals. You can be one of them.

After reading this chapter, you have learned

> ➤ how your values and beliefs can be better understood to bring you personal success.

> ➤ how your personal belief system affects who you are and how you are perceived.

> ➤ what you can do to change your personal beliefs to bring you more success and self-confidence.

> ➤ how to harness the power of self-belief to increase your potential and achieve success.

JOURNAL

Thinking about new ideas is helpful, but writing about them in a journal will help you understand them much better. You will be able to see how the ideas can relate to your own life. This journal focuses on what your ideal days would be like; a diary, in contrast, is about what your day actually was.

Learn about success, values, beliefs, and behavior by answering the following journal questions.

1. Describe the most successful person you know. What makes this person successful, in your opinion?

_____

_____

_____

_____

_____

_____

_____

_____

_____

_____

_____

2. From whom did you learn your most important values? How were the values taught to you?

_____

_____

_____

_____

_____

_____

_____

_____

_____

3. Give a personal example of positive thoughts or beliefs that influenced your actions.

_____

_____

_____

_____

_____

_____

_____

_____

_____

_____

4. Describe (a) a behavior that you would like to change and (b) how you might use positive self-talk to help you change the behavior.

_____

_____

_____

_____

_____

_____

_____

_____

_____

_____

_____

_____

_____

_____

_____

_____

_____

_____

_____

Chapter 2

Setting Realistic Goals

Did you ever set out on a weekend afternoon for a walk or drive with no clear destination in mind? You changed direction at random, perhaps saw some interesting things, perhaps not. When you got home, you couldn't really say whether you had accomplished anything or not.

> Life is a journey: if you don't have a map and a plan and a timetable, you will get lost.
>
> PHILLIP C. MCGRAW, AUTHOR OF *LIFE STRATEGIES*

Wandering around might be a fine way to spend an afternoon, but it won't really do for a lifetime. Yet many people live their lives this way—reacting to chance events, letting things happen to them, drifting from one thing to another. In 20, 40, or 60 years, they may realize that they've used up a lot of their time on earth and have little to show for it. People who can point to achievements and successes generally are those who

take charge of their lives. They realize that they are responsible for themselves. They understand their own values and abilities. They decide what they want, and they go after it.

If you are not like this, you may envy people who are. Everyone knows a few people who from an early age knew exactly what they wanted of life—to be a model or a mechanic or a nurse, for example. Having such clear goals helped these people focus their efforts and achieve what they wanted.

You too can take charge of your life and determine its direction. You have already started this process in Chapter 1.

AP/WIDE WORLD PHOTOS

Extraordinary accomplishments often start with a dream. Steve Fossett dreamed of being the first person to circle the world alone in a balloon. In 2002, on his sixth attempt, he finally accomplished his goal.

Identifying Your Goals

A good way to start identifying your goals is to think about your deepest wishes and dreams. Perhaps you've always longed to be a dancer, visit China, or own your own home. Maybe you want to have three children, be governor of your state, or start your own business.

Perhaps you haven't thought about your dreams in a long time. If that's the case, try asking yourself these questions: If you had only one year left to live, what would you do? If you were granted three wishes, what would they be? If you were guaranteed success in anything you chose to do, what would you do?

Goals: Challenging and Realistic

Your dreams can be the source of many of your goals. People whose achievements are extraordinary often started with dreams that may have seemed out of their reach. By focusing on their dreams, they were able to concentrate their energies on achieving them, one step at a time.

Being realistic doesn't necessarily mean giving up dreams that appear to be long shots. Your goals should be realistic, taking into account your unique talents and abilities. Yet they should also be challenging and require effort to achieve. If your goals are too easily achieved, you are not realizing your full potential. You can do more.

Types of Goals

Do you have dreams and goals for each aspect of your life? Goals can be thought of as personal, educational, professional, and community service.

Personal Goals

Personal goals relate to your family or private life. You may want to increase your strength, lose ten pounds, get along better with your spouse, or learn to play the electric guitar. Improving your relationships with family and friends and improving yourself in personal ways are the general objectives of personal goals.

Educational Goals

Educational goals relate to your efforts to learn more and improve your educational credentials. They may take the form of learning about something new, for example, learning how to use a spreadsheet program. Or the goals may relate to certificates, diplomas, and degrees that you want to earn or schools you want to attend.

Professional Goals

Your objectives for your work life are professional goals. Professional goals may be broad, for example, becoming a salesperson or earning $50,000 a year. Or the goals may be more specific. You may want to pass a licensing exam in a particular field or get a job at a specific company.

Community Service Goals

Community service goals are related to improving conditions in your neighborhood, town, or city. Examples are helping homeless people, giving kids the opportunity to play team sports, participating in a parent-teacher organization, and bringing meals to housebound people. Achieving community service goals benefits the community, but it also gives you the satisfaction of accomplishing something yourself.

Length of Time to Achieve Goals

Some personal, educational, professional, and community service goals can be achieved in a month. Others might take a decade. When you are setting goals, it's helpful to think about how much time you will need to achieve them (see Figure 2-1). Short-term goals are those that can be achieved in a relatively brief period of time—a year or less. Intermediate-term goals can be achieved in one to five years. Long-term goals take at least five years to accomplish.

> Service to others is the rent you pay for your room here on earth.
>
> MUHAMMAD ALI,
> BOXING CHAMPION

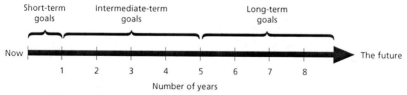

Figure 2-1: Short-term goals take a year or less to achieve, intermediate-term goals take from one to five years, and long-term goals take more than five years to accomplish.
AP/WIDE WORLD PHOTOS/DENNIS COOK

Note that long- and intermediate-term goals can often be thought of as a series of short-term goals. Earning an academic degree, diploma, or certificate is a long- or intermediate-term goal; each course you pass is a short-term goal that contributes to your objective.

Six Rules for Stating Goals

Thinking about your goals is not enough. It's important to write them down. Stating your goals helps you focus on them. Studies have shown that people who write down their goals are far more likely to achieve them than people who do not. When you state your goals, you should keep the following six rules in mind:

1. *Express your goals in positive language.* For example, "I will change my eating habits to maintain a weight of 120 pounds," rather than "I will not eat candy or cookies." Or "I will complete the report ahead of schedule," rather than "I won't be late for another report." When writing goals, you will find that positive language has the same beneficial effects as positive self-talk.

2. *Make your goals as specific as possible.* Avoid vague, general language like "I would like to travel." Instead, be specific and say something like "I will vacation in Aruba." Making goals specific helps you focus your efforts on achieving them.

3. *Make your goals measurable.* For example, suppose you want to save some money. How will you know whether you've reached your goal? When you've saved $100? $1,000? You have to have some way to measure whether you've achieved your goal. If you say you want to save $1,000 of your part-time earnings, you have a measurable goal. When you state a goal, ask yourself, "What do I want to accomplish? How will I know that I have accomplished it?" Your goal will be measurable if you can respond to these questions.

4. *Set yourself a deadline.* When do you want to achieve this goal? In two months? In two years? Whatever the answer, commit yourself to a time frame. Decide when you will start and when you will be done.

5. *Have a variety of goals.* It's important not to channel your efforts toward only one goal or one type of goal. If all your goals are professional, for example, you will find yourself neglecting other aspects of your life. Try

to achieve a balance of personal, educational, professional, community service, short-term, and long-term goals.

6. *Make your goals your own.* Having others set goals for you, even well-meaning people like parents, spouses, and friends, means that the goals are not truly your own. Your goals must be just that—yours. That way, you'll be committed to achieving them. Accomplishing your goals ought to give you pleasure and satisfaction.

Creating an Action Plan

> Light tomorrow with today.
>
> ELIZABETH BARRETT BROWNING,
> 19TH-CENTURY BRITISH POET

If you wanted to reach a specific place in downtown Kansas City, a street map of the city or directions from MapQuest.com would be very helpful. But suppose you used the wrong map or no directions at all. You'd probably get lost and become very frustrated. In the same way, once you've decided on your goals—your destination—you need to plan how you'll reach them. A written action plan will help you focus your efforts and reach your goals without getting lost along the way. ■

What Are Your Goals?

Purpose: This exercise will ask you to fine-tune personal goals that you have for yourself. Use the chart below to record your personal, educational, professional, and community service goals. Remember to classify goals as either short-term (one year or less to accomplish), intermediate-term (one to five years), or long-term (more than five years to achieve). You may have more than one goal or no goals in a particular category.

Personal Goals

Short-term: *Stay healthy and fit*

Intermediate-term: _____

Long-term: *Get married and have a family*

Professional Goals

Short-term: _Get a job during intersession._

Intermediate-term: _Get an internship_

Long-term: _Get a good job where I can support myself_

Educational Goals

Short-term: _Keep my scholarship and maintain a high GPA_

Intermediate-term: _Graduate with my BS in HR_

Long-term: _Go to graduate school_

Community Service Goals

Short-term: _Go to a Habitat build_

Intermediate-term: _Get into the ISP service trip I want_

Long-term: _Be a leader on a service trip_

News & Views

New Year's Resolutions

New Year's Day is the traditional time for setting goals. After a holiday season in which people often eat, drink, and party too much, New Year's is the time when many people resolve to change something about their lives.

What do people resolve to do? MyGoals.com, an Internet site devoted to goal-setting, issues annual statistics on New Year's resolutions. The people who run this site base their breakdown of types of resolutions on the goal-setting activity on the Web site. According to their data, in 2003, career-oriented goals were the most common, followed by health and fitness goals.

"Jobs are what's on everybody's mind, period," said Greg Helmstetter, chief executive officer of myGoals.com. "The dramatic increase in work-related goals is not just about getting jobs but, in particular, doing well at current jobs," said Helmstetter. "People are focusing on acquiring new skills. . . . It's a real sign of the times."

Source: "New Trends for 2003 New Year's Resolutions," http://www.myGoals.com/about/pressRelease010.html, accessed January 23, 2003.

Prepare an Action Plan

Purpose: This exercise will help you to turn your goals into action. Refer to your goals statement and select three of your most important intermediate- or long-term goals. Using the Action Plan form below, create an action plan for these goals.

Action plan: intermediate- or long-term goals

1. Intermediate- or long-term goal: Graduate with BS in HR
    To be accomplished by: @ Spring 2017

    Step 1: Keep scholarship
    Results needed: Good grades + High GPA
    To be accomplished by: End of first year

    Step 2: Stay with all HR courses
    Results needed: take all necessary courses
    To be accomplished by: Graduation

    Step 3: Complete all business courses
    Results needed: maintain the required GPA to get minor
    To be accomplished by: graduation

    Step 4: Stay out of trouble
    Results needed: no citations
    To be accomplished by: graduation.

2. Intermediate- or long-term goal: Get a good job
    To be accomplished by: N/A

    Step 1: Graduate with good GPA and HR degree
    Results needed: Good grades
    To be accomplished by: Spring 2017

Step 2: _Business minor_
Results needed: _Take + pass required courses_
To be accomplished by: _____

Step 3: _Spanish minor_
Results needed: _____
To be accomplished by: _____

Step 4: _Internship_
Results needed: _____
To be accomplished by: _Summer of ~~step~~ junior year_

3. Intermediate- or long-term goal: _Get into ISP_
   To be accomplished by: _Freshman year_

Step 1: _apply ~~to get~~_
Results needed: _interview_
To be accomplished by: _____

Step 2: _~~get~~ interview_
Results needed: _____
To be accomplished by: _____

Step 3: _get desired trip_
Results needed: _____
To be accomplished by: _____

Step 4: _Raise funds_
Results needed: _____
To be accomplished by: _____

When preparing an action plan, think about your long-term goals first. In other words, start by knowing where you want to wind up. Let's say, for example, that Elena wants to open her own specialty clothing shop. First she decides that she wants to accomplish this within seven years. With that target in mind, Elena plans the steps she must take to open the shop. First she plans to work in a large clothing store for five years to get experience. At the same time, she will take courses at night in fashion merchandising, accounting, and other business subjects. She will also save 10 percent of her income each year toward the expense of starting a business. At the end of five years, Elena plans to look for a job in a small specialty shop in order to get more experience. During the two years before she opens the shop, she will save 15 percent of her income.

Elena has created an action plan for one of her long-term goals. Essentially, the steps she took were:

1. stating a long-term goal in specific terms and giving it a time frame.
2. breaking down the goal into short-term goals, or steps, that will lead to achieving the long-term goal.
3. indicating specific results of the short-term goals in order to monitor progress.
4. setting deadlines for the short-term goals.

If you follow these steps for each of your intermediate- or long-term goals, you will have an action plan for each goal. A plan for a short-term goal would skip step 2. The plan should be written so you can monitor your progress toward achieving your goals.

Reaching Your Goals

Making an action plan to achieve your goals is an important step. But to make progress, you will have to work hard, keep your goals in view, and persevere, even when you run into problems. Some people have trouble taking the first step toward a goal, and others make progress and then give up when they reach a plateau. Resist the temptation to stop when goals get tough. Some people need to supplement their inner motivation with help from family, friends, and support groups. Some people must come to grips with their feelings about failure and success. Others lack the flexibility to change and adapt to new situations. Finally, all of us can learn to improve our chances for success from naturally optimistic people.

Doug Blevins

COURTESY OF AP/WORLDWIDE PHOTOS

It is not unusual for a child to dream of a career in professional sports. Although few children grow up to achieve this dream, Doug Blevins did. Blevins, the kicking coach for the Miami Dolphins, has achieved his childhood goal despite having a disabling disease, cerebral palsy.

As a boy in Abingdon, Virginia, Blevins told his skeptical family and friends that one day he would be in the National Football League. Although he was on crutches at the time, he got involved in peewee football. When he was in junior high, he watched films of the local high school team's games and thought he saw problems with their kicking game. Blevins wrote to the kicking coach of the Dallas Cowboys, Ben Agajanian, asking for advice. Agajanian sent him coaching notes and tapes to study.

Thus Blevins's coaching career was launched. His first job was in high school as assistant student coach for the football team. Later, he got an athletic scholarship and part-time job as a student coach at Emory & Henry College and Tennessee State University. After graduating, he taught kicking skills from his wheelchair to a wide range of players from high school teams to the World Football League. "Not having actually kicked has helped me, because I don't bring a lot of bad mechanics or techniques to the game," says Blevins.

Finally, in 1994, Blevins achieved his dream: he was hired as a kicking consultant for an NFL team, the New York Jets. Later, he worked with players from the New England Patriots. In 1997, Blevins joined the Miami Dolphins as a full-time kicking coach.

During his years with the Miami Dolphins, Blevins has coached kicker Olindo Mare, whose career field goal accuracy is now 84.5 percent—the second best in NFL history. "A lot of people see Doug for the first time and wonder, 'How can this guy know anything about kicking?'" says Mare. "But what they don't know is how much film he has watched, how much he has studied about kicking, and how much experience he has in the business."

During off-seasons, Blevins speaks to the disabled, telling them to follow their dreams. "Don't listen to what everyone else says," Blevins advises. "You've got to follow your heart and do what you are capable of doing."

Source: Metzger's Miami Dolphin News, June 4, 1997; "Blevins Tutors Kickers From Wheelchair," Associated Press, August 3, 1997; Allison Burke, "Willing and Able: Cerebral Palsy Couldn't Keep Doug Blevins from a Place in Pro Football," *People,* September 8, 1997; Bethany Broadwell, "Blevins Coaches His Way toward Goal," iCan News Service, November 22, 2001, at http://www.ican.com/news, accessed January 23, 2003; "Coaching Staff Profile," Miami Dolphins Web site, http://www.miamidolphins.com/lockerroom/coachingstaff/coachingstaff_blevins_d.asp, accessed January 23, 2003.

Taking the First Step

Old habits and ways of living are powerful forces. Taking the first step toward a major goal can be hard. But procrastinating, or postponing a task that ought to be done now, is the sure way to fail to reach a goal. People who procrastinate usually have a "good" reason.

> You'll always miss 100 percent of the shots you do not take.
>
> WAYNE GRETZKY, HOCKEY PLAYER

Postponing a task will not make it easier. Rather, when you are tempted to put off something important, you should carefully think about what is holding you back. You may be feeling shy, indecisive, fearful, negative, or bad about yourself. You feel you can't do something, so you don't do it. The result is inaction.

To overcome procrastination, you can change your beliefs and you can change your behavior. We've already discussed the power of positive self-talk in improving your self-belief. If you are a procrastinator, now is the time for some serious conversation with yourself.

> The best way to get something done is to begin.
>
> ANONYMOUS

Tips for Getting Started

One technique you can use is visualization. Visualization means imagining what it would be like to have already reached a goal. What scene do you picture? What sounds do you hear? How are the people around you reacting to you? Imagining the future can compel us to do things now, in order to create the kind of future we want. Visualizing your success gives you a powerful mental boost to get started.

Another approach for people who procrastinate is to start by doing a little bit. There are several techniques you can use to get yourself started on a task.

> Set a deadline for getting started. By focusing on a starting date, you will find the energy to begin because you have made a commitment to yourself.

> List small tasks—that will take only a minute or two—that can get you started. Then do the first one.

> Do anything in connection with the goal. If you have to write letters and can't get started, then ease into the task by looking up the addresses or preparing the envelopes first.

> Assign a short period of time during which you will work on the goal. For example, tell yourself that for the next five minutes you will do things that relate to the goal.

> Do the worst thing first. Sometimes tackling the hardest part and getting it done opens up the way to achieving the goal.

Any one of these approaches, in combination with positive self-talk and visualization, can help you get started.

Using the Mastery Approach

Many people get off to a good start when they try to work on their goals, and then they get bogged down and give up. They experience a short burst of progress, followed by a period of being on a plateau, during which nothing seems to happen. A perfect example of this is a man whose goal is to learn a new sport. At first, he makes rapid progress. But then, instead of continuing to improve, he reaches a plateau. For weeks or even months, his skill level remains the same. Finally, another burst of progress occurs, and his mastery of the sport increases.

> To accomplish great things, we must not only act, but also dream; not only plan, but also believe.
>
> ANATOLE FRANCE,
> 20TH-CENTURY
> FRENCH WRITER

The secret of the mastery approach is to expect and accept that you will reach plateaus and stop progressing. When this happens, don't give up! Instead, persist, understanding that plateauing is natural and that you will eventually make more progress.

Motivating Yourself

How do you keep yourself moving toward a goal even when you've reached a plateau? How can you motivate yourself to act in ways that will keep you striving and trying? Motivation is having the energy to work toward a goal. It is made up of the needs and incentives that make us act in particular ways. Motivation can be complex, but we will consider two aspects that are particularly relevant to achievement.

First, motivation that comes from within is called intrinsic motivation. When you are intrinsically motivated, you do something because you want to and you enjoy it. Let's say you like to do aerobic exercises. They make you feel good. You are intrinsically motivated to exercise.

You may have a friend, however, who knows she should exercise but thinks it's boring. You want your friend to take an aerobics class with you. To persuade her, you think of some extrinsic motivation, which is an outside reward for behavior. You offer your friend an exercise outfit and a ride to class. These extrinsic motivations may be enough to get your friend to come with you, at least for a while. Over time, though, the value of extrinsic motivation decreases. After a few weeks the extrinsic rewards may lose their power to get your friend to aerobics. However, if your friend has discovered that aerobics is fun and makes her feel and look great, then she will have acquired intrinsic motivation to exercise. Your rewards will no longer be necessary because your friend is motivated from within to continue exercising.

> Fame or one's own self, which matters to one most? One's own self or things bought, which should count most?
>
> LAO-TZU, ANCIENT CHINESE PHILOSOPHER

In most situations, people have a combination of intrinsic and extrinsic motivations. Meg may enjoy learning how to use a computer (intrinsic) but she is also doing it to earn course credits (extrinsic). Psychologists have found that the best form of extrinsic motivation is praise. Unlike other extrinsic rewards, praise tends to increase a person's intrinsic motivation to do well.

If you are intrinsically motivated to achieve a goal, your chances of achieving it are good. Working on the goal is something you enjoy, so you don't look for excuses to stop. If your intrinsic motivation needs a boost, you can use positive self-talk and visualization to keep your energy high. Congratulate yourself on what you've accomplished so far, and imagine what it's going to be like when you reach your goal.

If you need some extrinsic motivation to keep you going, you can do two things:

> A failure is not always a mistake; it may simply be the best one can do under the circumstances. The real mistake is to stop trying.
>
> B. F. SKINNER, PSYCHOLOGIST

1. Set up a system of rewards for yourself. For example, when you accomplish one step toward a goal, reward yourself with something you enjoy. Just be careful not to let the reward become more important than doing the task.

2. Enlist the support of your family or friends. If you communicate your goals and successes, the pride that others feel in your accomplishments will provide powerful motivation for you to persevere.

Overcoming Fears

Fear often stands in the way of action. People are hampered by fear of many things. The two most important fears that can interfere with reaching a goal are fear of failure and fear of success.

What Motivates You?

Purpose: This exercise will help you to determine what motivates you to achieve your goals. Consider the three goals for which you prepared action plans. What will motivate you to accomplish these goals?

1. *Goal 1:*_____
   Your intrinsic motivation: _____
   Sources of extrinsic motivation:_____

2. *Goal 2:*_____
   Your intrinsic motivation: _____
   Sources of extrinsic motivation:_____

3. *Goal 3:*_____
   Your intrinsic motivation: _____
   Sources of extrinsic motivation:_____

You may think that fearing failure makes perfect sense. In a way, it does. No one likes to look stupid, incompetent, or ridiculous. Actually, it's our perception of failure that causes fear. Instead of seeing failure as a poor result or a temporary setback, we see failure as defeat and shame. If we remember that everyone fails at times, we can start putting failure in perspective. Out of failure can come valuable lessons for success.

However odd it sounds, people often fear success also. People who fear success are seldom aware of it. Yet they put obstacles in the way of achieving their goals. Why? They fear that success will bring new situations and new responsibilities they can't handle. Some may believe that they don't deserve to succeed. In fact, they probably can succeed. Most people tend to underestimate their abilities.

If fear is preventing you from achieving your goals, tell yourself this: "Fear is natural. I feel afraid, but I'm going to do this anyway."

Being Flexible

Life means change, and people who don't change their goals accordingly run into trouble. Suppose your family moves to another state or you become interested in another career. It would be foolish to persist in trying to reach goals that are no longer relevant to you. Goals and action plans are not carved in stone. When your situation changes, be flexible and change your goals and action plans to suit your new circumstances.

Being Less Than Perfect

People who are perfectionists often get bogged down in trying to reach their goals. They demand perfection of themselves. Nothing they do is ever good enough. They are always in a hurry. Most important, perfectionists can't acknowledge that they can make mistakes. They must appear to be strong at all times.

On the other hand, people who reach their goals tend to be more relaxed about themselves. They acknowledge that they are human and have faults. They make mistakes, but they do as well as they can. They realize the importance of pleasing themselves. They are flexible and relaxed and open to new situations and people. These are the people who have the inner resources to succeed.

The Importance of Hope

Psychologists are finding that hope plays an important role in achieving success in life. A study of 3,920 college freshmen showed that the level of hope at the start of school was a better predictor of their college grades than previous performance on standardized tests or their high school grade point average. Dr. Charles R. Snyder, a psychologist at the University of Kansas, says, "Students with high hope set themselves higher goals and know how to work to attain them."

> The man who makes no mistakes does not usually make anything.
>
> EDWARD JOHN PHELPS, 19TH-CENTURY LAWYER AND DIPLOMAT

To Dr. Snyder, hope is more than the feeling that everything will be okay. Rather, he defines having hope as believing that you have both the will and the way to accomplish your goals. In other words, people with commitment and self-belief are hopeful people. People who are naturally hopeful are fortunate. But others can learn hopeful ways of thinking. To imitate the mental habits of hopeful people, you can

> ➤ turn to friends for help in achieving your goals.
> ➤ use positive self-talk.
> ➤ believe that things will get better.
> ➤ be flexible enough to change your action plans when necessary.
> ➤ be flexible enough to change your goals when necessary.
> ➤ focus on the short-term goals you need to achieve in order to reach your long-term goal.

ELEMENTS OF EXCELLENCE

After reading this chapter, you have learned

> ➤ how to develop effective, measurable goals that will lead you to personal success.
> ➤ what steps can be taken to create an action plan for completing your goals.
> ➤ techniques that will help you effectively reach your goals and measure their impact.
> ➤ how being flexible and open to a changing landscape will assist you in successful goal completion.

Getting Up to Speed

The Internet has several Web sites that provide good goal-setting guidance and advice.

> MyGoals.com is one of the Internet's leading goal-setting sites. According-ing to the Web site, "MyGoals.com walks you through a comprehensive, step-by-step goal-setting process for any goal, whether it's short-term or long-term, easy or difficult, practical or lofty."

> Mind Tools Ltd. is a British company that sells software to help people think more productively. Their Web site offers solid general advice on goal setting and tips for achieving goals, **http://www.mindtools.com**. They also offer goal-setting software.

> College Net and College Opportunities On-Line can help you to set or achieve educational goals by providing a search tool for information about colleges, **http://www.collegenet.com** and **http://nces.ed.gov**.

> If your educational goals include attending a community college, you can check out two sites that provide information on community colleges throughout the United States: **http://www.mcli.dist.maricopa.edu/** and **http://www.utoledo.edu**. Instead of going to a specific Internet address such as these, you can do a search using the key word *goal-setting* or key words having to do with your specific goals. For example, you can do a search on a particular career, a specific type of volunteer work, or the name of a school you're interested in attending.

JOURNAL

Answer the following questions.

1. In this chapter, you listed your personal, professional, educational, and community service goals. Of all the goals you listed, which is most im-portant to you? Why?

_____

_____

_____

_____

_____

_____

_____

_____

_____

_____

_____

_____

_____

2. Visualize yourself when you achieve your most important goal. Describe what your life will be like.

_____

_____

_____

_____

_____

_____

_____

_____

_____

_____

_____

3. What is the biggest obstacle you think you will face in achieving this goal? How can you overcome this obstacle?

_____

_____

_____

_____

_____

_____

_____

_____

_____

_____

_____

_____

4. List people who can help or support your effort to reach this goal.

_____

_____

_____

_____

_____

_____

_____

_____

_____

_____

_____

_____

_____

_____

_____

Chapter 3

Improving Your Thinking Skills

Have you ever done poorly on an exam because you had a cold? Have you ever been unable to solve a problem because you were too anxious about it? These common experiences show that our ability to think is affected by our physical and emotional well-being. When we feel good about ourselves, both emotionally and physically, our ability to think improves.

Studies have shown that all of us have far more brain power than we use. We can improve our ability to think by tapping into some of that unused power. If we understand how the brain works, we can sharpen our thinking

COURTESY OF CORBIS

People in all walks of life solve problems and think creatively. Astronauts Ellen Ochoa and Donald McMonagle use their education and NASA training to meet the challenges of space flight.

skills. In this chapter, you will learn about the brain and you will improve your ability to remember, think critically, solve problems, and think creatively.

The Brain

Make two fists and place them together with your thumbs on top and your arms touching from wrist to elbow. You have just made a crude model of the human brain. The brain, a three-pound organ, is the complex director of all of your body's activities.

The human brain's ability to deal with complex perceptions, thoughts, and feelings is the key to our success as a species. We cannot run as fast as a cheetah or see our prey with eyes as sharp as an eagle's, but we use our brains to make up for our physical limitations. Humans survive because our brains constantly filter the information coming in from the environment. The brain tells us what is safe to ignore—most of what's around us. It tells us what we must pay attention to. Every encounter with something new means that the brain must try to fit the new information into an existing pattern of neurons or else change the pattern to make room for the new thing. Because humans learn and remember, we have thrived.

However, your brain can pay attention to only one train of conscious thought at a time. It is always getting rid of excess information through the process of forgetting. What does the brain pay attention to? It pays attention to things that have meaning to you (information that connects to an existing network of neurons) or things that arouse feelings (information that makes you afraid, happy, or angry).

We can use this very basic understanding of how the human brain works to improve our ability to remember, think logically, solve problems, and think creatively.

Remembering

One of the most basic functions of the brain is to remember. Without memory, other learning and thinking skills would be impossible. Your brain stores a vast amount of information in memory. This ranges from important

> I will stuff your head with brains. I cannot tell you how to use them, however; you must find that out for yourself. (The Wizard of Oz to the Scarecrow, who asked for brains.)
>
> L. FRANK BAUM, AMERICAN WRITER

> Iron rusts from disuse, stagnant water loses its purity, and in cold weather becomes frozen; even so does inaction sap the vigors of the mind.
>
> LEONARDO DA VINCI, RENAISSANCE ITALIAN ARTIST, MUSICIAN, ENGINEER, AND SCIENTIST

information such as a friend's appearance to trivial information like the sound of the doorbell in your last apartment or house.

Most psychologists think of memory as having three stages: (1) sensory memory, (2) short-term memory, and (3) long-term memory. Figure 3-1 is a diagram of the three-stage model of memory.

Everything you perceive is registered in sensory memory, the first stage of memory. The material in sensory memory lasts less than a couple of seconds while your brain processes it, looking for what's important. Then most of it disappears.

Some material in sensory memory reaches the second stage, short-term memory. To make it into short-term memory, the new material is matched with information you already have stored, and a meaningful association or pattern is made. For example, when you see a T, you immediately recognize it as the letter *T*. You would recognize it whether it was a lowercase t, an italic t, an uppercase T, or a handwritten T. If you did not have these associations for the letter T, you would have much more difficulty placing it in short-term memory.

The material in short-term memory is the information we are currently using. The capacity of short-term memory is small—on average, about seven meaningful units of information. And short-term memory usually doesn't last more than 20 seconds. To make it last longer, repetition helps. For example, if you are lost and someone is giving you directions, you should repeat them to fix them in your memory. But if someone interrupts you, you will probably confuse or forget the directions.

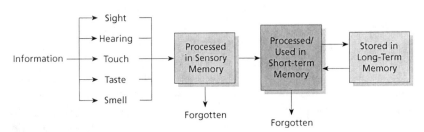

Figure 3-1: The three stages of memory are sensory memory, short-term memory, and long-term memory. Our five senses perceive information from our environment, which is processed in sensory memory. Only the important information is sent on to short-term memory. There it is processed and used. Then the information is either forgotten or sent to long-term memory for storage. When the information is needed, it is retrieved from long-term memory, if it can be found.

Some material in short-term memory makes it into the third stage, long-term memory, which lasts much longer than short-term memory. Long-term memories are those we don't need at the moment but have stored. In fact, long-term memory is often compared to a complicated filing system, index, or database. The way memories are stored affects the ease with which we can retrieve them. In general, we store new memories by associating them with old memories. For example, if we see a new shade of blue we may associate it with other shades of blue we know or with a blue object.

The capacity of long-term memory seems limitless. Even after a full life of remembering, people have room to store more information in long-term memory. Much of what we "forget" is still actually in long-term memory, but we have trouble getting it out.

> The true art of memory is the art of attention.
>
> SAMUEL JOHNSON,
> 18TH-CENTURY
> ENGLISH AUTHOR

Improving Your Memory

There are several techniques you can use to improve your short-term and long-term memory. Of course, one time-honored way to improve your memory is to write yourself lists and notes. However, you can learn other purely mental aids to memory that take advantage of how the brain works. These include repetition, organization, and mnemonics.

Repetition

Repetition is an effective way to improve your short-term memory. Going over something again and again in your head—or even better, out loud—will help you keep it in short-term memory long enough to use it.

Organization

Organizing material can help both your short-term and long-term memory. To help keep something in short-term memory, you can organize it into seven or fewer chunks. A grocery list of 20 items, for instance, can be "chunked" into produce, dairy, deli, meats, packaged foods, paper products, and cleaning products.

The way you organize material for long-term storage will help you when you need to retrieve it. One way is to make meaningful associations between the new information you are memorizing and other information you already know. For example, if you are trying to remember to buy fish at the supermarket, you can associate it with the meal you're planning to cook. Associations need not involve only words. You can associate new information with music, sounds, images, places, people, and so on.

The Nun Study: The Importance of Mental Exercise

"Use it or lose it" is a familiar saying that may turn out to be true in regard to the brain. A study of 678 nuns has provided insights about why some people live to a great age with their minds lively and intact, while others suffer from Alzheimer's disease or other forms of dementia.

The School Sisters of Notre Dame are a good group to study from a scientific point of view. They do not smoke, drink very little, and get good health care. In addition, they live in similar communities all their lives. The sisters keep mentally and physically active well into old age. The Nun Study, as it is known, is conducted by Dr. David Snowdon of the University of Kentucky.

Each year, Dr. Snowdon and his colleagues test the nuns' memory, concentration, and language ability. For example, the nuns are asked to recall words they have seen on flash cards and to name as many items in a category as they can in one minute.

Dr. Snowdon also analyzed essays the nuns wrote decades earlier when they entered the convent. These autobiographies provided evidence of the young sisters' thinking and language abilities. The researchers measured the "idea density"—the number of ideas in ten written words—and the grammatical complexity of the essays. They also looked for words that indicated a positive or a negative mental outlook. The essays gave Dr. Snowdon a way to compare the nuns' mental skills in their youth and in old age.

Much to his surprise, Dr. Snowdon found that the sisters who had shown a positive outlook in their essays lived longer than those whose essays showed a negative outlook. Furthermore, those whose essays had high idea density and grammatical complexity were far less likely than the others to develop symptoms of Alzheimer's disease in old age. The results of the study suggest that people who exercise their minds may protect themselves from declining mental function as they age. Sisters who had taught school, for example, showed better mental health in old age than those who cooked and cleaned in the convent. Of course, Alzheimer's disease is partially caused by genetic factors, so in many cases it may not be possible to prevent the disease. Still, the educated nuns whose lives had been mentally active may have developed extra brain capacity—more connections among neurons. These extra connections gave them a surplus they could draw on, even as Alzheimer's disease may have been developing.

This suggests that the average person should choose new and stimulating things to do or study throughout life. A personal trainer could take up painting.

A computer technician might learn a new language. Even simple activities like brain teasers, crossword puzzles, and jigsaw puzzles can help expand the brain's capacity.

Source: Michael D. Lemonick and Alice Park, "The Nun Study: How One Scientist and 678 Sisters Are Helping Unlock the Secrets of Alzheimer's Disease, Time Pacific, May 14, 2001, http://www.time.com/tim/pacific/magazine/20010514/cover1.html; Jay Copp, "This Is for the Benefit of Those Who Come after Us," Our Sunday Visitor, June 17, 2001, http://www.osv.com/periodicals/show-article.asp?pid=313; "Creative Challenges," 1998, Creative Thinking Web site, http://www.sunmoments.com/DT/vlil, all accessed January 28, 2003.

Mnemonics

"I before E except after C and when it sounds like A, as in neighbor or in weigh" has helped children learn one of the rules of English spelling for years. Devices that help people remember are called mnemonics. Mnemonics can be poems, like this example, or they can be acronyms—the first letter of each item to be memorized.

In addition to rhymes and acronyms, there are mnemonic systems that can be used to help memorize information. One system, called the pegword method, involves learning a jingle that contains words corresponding to the numbers 1 through 10:

> 1 is a bun; 2 is a shoe; 3 is a tree; 4 is a door; 5 is a hive; 6 is sticks; 7 is heaven; 8 is a gate; 9 is swine; 10 is a hen.

After repeating this jingle a few times, you will be able to count to 10 by pegwords: bun, shoe, tree, door, and so on. Then you can visually associate items you need to remember with the pegwords. For example, if the first item on your list is a notebook, you can imagine a notebook sandwiched on a bun. Later, when you need to remember the list, the ten pegwords will serve as clues to the items. The numbers will help you keep track of how many items you must remember.

Thinking Critically

Memory is one form of thought; another is critical thinking. When you think critically, you are evaluating what's true and are making judgments. To do this, you must be able to reason, or think logically. You must also be able to distinguish fact from opinion.

Logic

Whether you are aware of it or not, you use logic hundreds of times a day. When you are hungry, you decide to eat. When you need to know the time, you look at a clock. When it's chilly, you put on a jacket. In all these cases, you have used a logical sequence of steps in thinking. One type of logical thinking is called deductive reasoning. In deductive reasoning, the conclusion that is reached is true premise is true. Let's consider an example of deductive reasoning.

> Take time to think. . . . It is the source of power.

Premise	When it rains, the street gets wet.
Premise	It is raining.
Conclusion	The street is wet.

You can see from this example that you use deductive reasoning all the time without even being aware of it. When you make a decision, however, you are often aware of your thought process. Let's say you must decide whether your car needs servicing. You might follow this train of thought:

Premise	If the car leaks oil, it needs servicing.
Premise	The car leaks oil.
Conclusion	The car needs servicing.

The conclusion in deductive reasoning is always true if the premises are true.

A type of thinking in which the conclusion is not always true is called inductive reasoning. In inductive reasoning, the conclusion drawn is probably true. Here's an example of inductive reasoning:

Premise	Coworkers Francine and Bill have the same last name.
Premise	Francine and Bill leave the office together every day.
Conclusion	Francine and Bill are married.

While it is possible that Francine and Bill are married, this conclusion may not be true. Francine and Bill may be sister and brother, mother and son, daughter and father, or cousins. In fact, Francine and Bill may not be related at all—they may simply have the same last name.

Fact or Opinion?

To distinguish between fact and opinion, think logically. Evaluate the material and sort out the reasonable from the emotional or illogical. Look for inconsistencies and evidence. Above all, trust your own ability to distinguish logical facts and ideas from opinions and assumptions. One area in which Americans have had a lot of practice in sorting fact from opinion is advertising. Think of your favorite commercial and try to sort out the facts from the assumptions.

Solving Problems

Problem solving is another important thinking skill. To be a good problem solver, you must be able to think critically. In addition, recognize that problems often have an emotional component that affects your ability to deal with them.

> It is the mark of an educated mind to be able to entertain a thought without accepting it.
>
> ARISTOTLE, ANCIENT GREEK PHILOSOPHER

Proactive versus Reactive Attitudes

Let's consider Steve, who is having trouble getting along with a coworker. Steve thinks, "It's unfair that I have to deal with him. He shouldn't be my problem. Anyway, it's his fault. I don't have the time to work things out." With this attitude, how likely is it that Steve will be able to solve the problem?

Now Steve pulls himself together and tells himself that he will take full responsibility for this problem. He will do what's necessary to solve it. Steve will even enlist the help of others, if necessary. Since he believes that he can solve the problem, his chances of success are increased. These two attitudes toward problem solving can be characterized as reactive or proactive. A reactive approach is essentially negative. A person with a reactive attitude feels incapable of solving the problem and tries to blame someone else. In contrast, a person with a proactive attitude takes responsibility and is committed to solving the problem.

So before we undertake the steps involved in thinking through and solving a problem, it's important to have a proactive attitude.

The Destructive Power of Negative Attitudes

Having a negative attitude can really cause havoc in your day-to-day success. As you have observed in others, being negative and acting the role of doomsayer is not productive. Unfortunately, it can be difficult to always be chipper and positive, as challenge and change are constants in any workplace. Be careful to not be the person at the workplace that everyone sees this way. Evaluate your attitude regularly.

Whatever It Takes

Lonnie G. Johnson

AP/WIDE WORLD PHOTOS/JOHN BAZEMORE

You may never have heard of a flow-actuated pulsator, but you certainly know it by its more common name—the Super Soaker. Invented in 1982 by engineer Lonnie G. Johnson, the high-powered water gun has become one of the most popular summer toys ever made.

Johnson, who grew up in Mobile, Alabama, was the third of six children. Even though he was told he didn't have what it takes to become an engineer, Johnson persevered. When he was a high school senior, his science project, a remote-controlled robot, won first place at a University of Alabama science fair. "Back then, robots were unheard of, so I was one of only a few kids in the country who had his own robot," said Johnson. Johnson went to college on math and military scholarships. He earned a bachelor's degree in mechanical engineering and a master's degree in nuclear engineering.

Johnson worked for NASA's Jet Propulsion Laboratory, helping to fit an atomic battery into the space probe Galileo. He also worked on the stealth bomber for the Air Force. In his free time, Johnson fooled around with things at home. While trying to invent a cooling system that didn't use Freon gas, Johnson rigged up some tubing and a nozzle in his bathroom. When he pressed the nozzle, a blast of water shot into the bathtub. Johnson thought, "This would make a great water gun."

The Super Soaker sold so well that in 1991 Johnson was able to form his own company, Johnson Research and Development. When asked what the key to success is, Johnson said, "Perseverance! There is no short, easy route to success." And when asked why he invented things, he replied, "I have these ideas, and they keep on coming."

Source: Tracie Newton, "Inventor Encourages Audience to Persevere in Quest for Dreams, Holds Up Own Life as Example," Athens Online, February 28, 1999, http://www.onlineathens. com/stories/022899/new_0228990002.shtml, accessed January 13, 2003; Susan Fineman, "Sometimes It Does Take a Rocket Scientist," Associated Press, February 13, 1999, http://www.invention-express.com/lonniejohnson.html, accessed January 13, 2003; William J. Broad, "Rocket Science, Served Up Soggy," *New York Times,* July 31, 2001, pp. D1, D7.

YOUR TURN 3-1

Approach Problems Proactively

Purpose: This exercise will help you to clarify an important personal question and will give you an effective strategy for brainstorming solutions.

Think of a problem you have—personal, school-related, or job-related— and answer the following questions.

1. Describe your problem in one sentence.

_____

_____

2. Write down all the reasons why you can't solve this problem.

_____

_____

_____

_____

3. Now imagine that you can successfully solve the problem. Write down all the factors that are driving you to solve this problem.

_____

_____

_____

_____

4. Write a positive message to yourself about your commitment to solving the problem.

_____

_____

_____

_____

The PrOACT Approach to Problem Solving

Now that we've decided on a proactive attitude to problem solving, let's consider the elements involved in solving a problem or making a decision. Many people approach problem solving by using the trial-and-error method. This means they try out solutions at random and use the first one that works. It's not very efficient, and the results are often poor.

A better approach has been devised by three Harvard University business professors and decision-making consultants. Essentially, they advise breaking down a problem and considering it one step at a time: problem, objectives, alternatives, consequences, and trade-offs—or PrOACT.

In the PrOACT approach, you break a problem into the five PrOACT elements and think about each one separately. Then you put your thoughts back together and make a smart choice.

1. _Problem._ First, you have to figure out just what the problem is. Your ability to solve a problem depends on how you define it. For example, is your problem deciding whether or not to buy a car, or deciding which car to buy?
2. _Objectives._ Solving a problem or making a decision should bring you closer to achieving your goals. In a problem-solving situation, therefore,

you need to know what your objectives are. For example, your objective could be to buy a vehicle that has room for your family of six, is reasonably priced, and gets good gas mileage.

3. *Alternatives.* What different courses of action can you think of? What solutions are there to your problem? Think of as many possible alternatives as you can.

4. *Consequences.* For each reasonable alternative you come up with, think through the possible consequences, or results. Which alternatives have consequences that match your objectives?

5. *Trade-offs.* Whatever solution you choose, there will be pros and cons. You need to evaluate the pros and cons and decide what trade-offs are acceptable. There is no perfect solution to a problem; even the best alternative has drawbacks.

Constructing a decision matrix, or grid, such as the one in Table 3-1, can help you frame the problem, explore alternatives, and make a good decision. Which car would be best for the family of six?

Thinking Creatively

What makes people creative? Intelligence, you may be surprised to learn, has little relation to creativity. Many highly intelligent people do not think creatively. Rather, creative people tend to be those who are intrinsically motivated. They choose to do what they do. Often they live or work in an environment that is stimulating and brings them into contact with other creative people. Creative people perform tasks without fear of being judged foolish. They are not afraid to make mistakes.

> To raise new questions, new possibilities, to regard old problems from a new angle requires creative imagination.
>
> ALBERT EINSTEIN, PHYSICIST

TABLE 3-1	Decision Matrix for Buying a Family Car		
	Alternatives		
Objectives	Sedan	Minivan	SUV
Seating	5	7	6
Approximate cost	$20,000	$20,000	$30,000
Gas mileage	28 mpg	25 mpg	13 mpg

Improving Your Creativity

Creativity does not depend on talent or intelligence. Rather, creativity depends on how we use our brains. Most of the techniques associated with improving creativity are based on using neglected modes of thinking. Since analytic, verbal, and sequential modes of thinking dominate in our society, creative breakthroughs often come about when people tap into other modes of thinking. The techniques described here have one thing in common: They all focus on getting us to change our routine thought processes.

Associative Thinking

Associative thinking is a method in which you let your mind wander from one thing to another, even seemingly unrelated matters, in order to get fresh insight on a problem. If you have ever used the Internet, wandering from Web site to Web site with the links provided, you have a good idea of how associative thinking works.

To use associative thinking, start with the problem or issue and think of a couple of key words. For example, if you must decide whether to go to school full-time or part-time, your key words might be *school* and *time*. Starting with those words, let your mind wander, and jot down words and thoughts as they come to you. Sometimes associative thinking triggers useful new connections in your mind.

Back-Burner Thinking

Occasionally, when you think too much about a problem, you get stuck. No matter how you rack your brain, nothing useful occurs to you. So you put the problem out of your mind. Some time later, as if from nowhere, you have a great insight. The problem is solved. What has happened? Essentially, although you've stopped thinking about the problem on a conscious level, your brain continues to work on it. You've put the problem on a "back burner." Back-burner thinking involves knowing when to stop thinking about a problem and let your unconscious mind take over.

You can improve the chances that back-burner thinking will help you solve a problem by following these tips:

> Think about your problem, but if you are getting nowhere, stop.
> Do something else, preferably something relaxing. If it's night, go to sleep.
> Return to the problem after the break.

When you start thinking about the problem again, you may have gained a new perspective.

Mind-Mapping

Mind-mapping is a creative technique that draws on the visual, intuitive thought processes that we often neglect when trying to solve a problem. In mind-mapping, you sketch your problem or topic and the thoughts that come to mind. The result is a drawing that represents your ideas (see Figure 3-2).

To draw a mind-map, follow these steps:

1. Draw a picture of the problem or issue in the center of a piece of paper.
2. Print key words and ideas, and connect these to the central drawing.
3. Use colors, images, symbols, and codes to emphasize important points.
4. Use associative thinking to come up with more ideas, and connect them with other parts of the mind-map.

When your mind-map is done, you can study it to find new relationships, insights, and ideas. Perhaps a pattern will emerge that can help you with the problem.

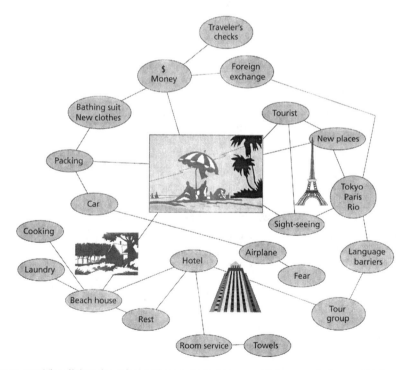

Figure 3-2: Visualizing the relationships among ideas and things can help you think creatively. You can draw a mind-map to show these connections.

Draw Your Own Mind-Map

Purpose: A mind-map is a powerful way to gain insight on a pressing issue in your life. This exercise asks you to practice this technique.

Think of a problem you have or an issue that interests you.

1. On a separate sheet of paper, draw a mind-map with a picture related to this problem or issue in the center.

2. Write key words and phrases about the problem or issue around the central drawing, and draw lines to show the connections among these ideas.

3. Use colors, symbols, images, and codes to emphasize important ideas.

4. Use associative thinking to add related ideas to your mind-map.

5. Study your mind-map. What patterns or ideas might help you with solving this problem or dealing with this issue?

Brainstorming

Someone once said that two heads are better than one. Taking this idea even further, brainstorming allows a group of people—preferably five to eight—to come up with as many ideas about a problem or issue as they can. To brainstorm effectively, people must not be critical of one another's ideas. Any idea, however far-fetched, is considered. Evaluating and judging will come later. Brainstorming can be used effectively in business situations in which groups of people share problems and goals.

Mindstorming

Mindstorming is similar to brainstorming, but you do it alone. Take a piece of paper, and at the top write your problem or issue of great concern. Then list 20 ways you can solve the problem or approach the issue. The first 10 ideas will probably come easily and seem obvious. However, don't judge your ideas yet. Let your imagination take over and write down 10 more ideas, however odd, that come to mind. Then review the list and choose the ideas that are most likely to solve your problem.

ELEMENTS OF EXCELLENCE

After reading this chapter, you have learned

> how the brain works, how it impacts memory, and techniques to improve your cognition.
> what the important tenets of critical thinking and problem solving are, and how to use them.
> why creative thinking will impact your personal success, and which techniques will unleash your creative abilities.

The Information Highway

Getting Up to Speed

Here are Web sites that have information on thinking skills, including memory and creative thinking:

> **http://www.mindtools.com.** Mind Tools Ltd. sells software to help people think more productively. Their Web site offers free information on improving thinking and memory skills.
> Visit the How Stuff Works Web site for an overview of how the brain works. **http://howstuffworks.com.**

Try the following key words to search for information on thinking skills: *memory techniques, mnemonics, critical thinking, problem solving, creativity.*

In addition, if you need help in solving a particular problem or thinking about a topic, search for the specific problem or topic that concerns you.

Last, do a search on any topic that interests you, and follow the links from one Web site to another. The links between sites are examples of associative thinking!

Answer the following journal questions.

1. What is your earliest memory of school? Why do you think you remember this event or thing?

_____

_____

_____

_____

_____

_____

_____

_____

_____

_____

_____

_____

2. How does your memory work to your advantage now? Are there things that you wish you could improve?

_____

_____

_____

_____

_____

_____

_____

_____

_____

_____

_____

_____

_____

_____

_____

3. In this chapter, you wrote about a problem that you have. Describe how you might use the PrOACT approach to solve this problem.

_____

_____

_____

_____

_____

_____

_____

_____

_____

_____

_____

_____

_____

_____

_____

4. Describe the most creative person you know. What makes this person creative, in your opinion?

_____

_____

_____

_____

_____

_____

_____

_____

_____

_____

_____

_____

_____

_____

_____

_____

Chapter 4

Staying Healthy

Take a look in a mirror. Do you see a healthy person with bright clear eyes and skin, fit and attractive, with lots of energy? If you do, you are probably already working hard at reaching your physical potential. But if that person in the mirror looks less than glowing, don't worry! There are many things you can do to improve your health and feel better mentally as well as physically.

> Happiness lies, first of all, in health.
>
> GEORGE WILLIAM CURTIS

If you have ever felt sick, you know the value of good health. When you are not feeling healthy, all aspects of your life suffer. You become unable to live up to your emotional, intellectual, and social potential. All of you suffers—not just your body.

What does it take to feel healthy and energetic? In this chapter, you will learn about the importance of eating a balanced diet in preventing disease and maintaining good health. You will learn about and assess in yourself the physical benefits of different types of exercise, sleep patterns and how you spend your energy. Also in this chapter will be the physical effects of drug use on the body and mind.

At 24, champion cyclist Lance Armstrong learned he had cancer that had spread to his lungs and brain. His physical well-being, which he had always taken for granted, was threatened. After treatment, Armstrong slowly returned to cycling. Eventually, he won the Tour de France, the world championship of bicycling, several times. Today the Lance Armstrong Foundation helps people manage and survive cancer.

AP/WIDE WORLD PHOTOS/TODD WARSHAW

Nutrients

Food provides nutrients, the substances your body uses for growth, maintenance, and repair, as well as for energy. Diets with too much or too little of a nutrient can be harmful to your health. In addition, the nutrients in foods affect your mind, mood, and energy level.

The major types of nutrients are protein, carbohydrates, fats, water, vitamins, and minerals. Table 4-1 shows the major nutrients, their functions in the body, and their food sources. The key to making sure you get all the necessary nutrients is to eat a wide variety of healthy foods.

Protein

Protein is a chemical substance that is part of all body cells. It has many functions, including growth and the maintenance and repair of tissue. Meat, fish, poultry, eggs, dairy products, nuts, and tofu are all sources of protein. In addition, beans can be sources of protein if they are eaten with grains.

Carbohydrates

Sugar, corn syrup, and other sweets are simple carbohydrates. Starches and grains are complex carbohydrates. Starches and grains also contain dietary fiber that aids digestion. In general, the more a complex carbohydrate food has been processed, the less fiber it has.

Fats

Fats provide concentrated storage of energy for the body. They also provide insulation and dissolve certain vitamins. There are two main types of fat:

1. Saturated fats are those that are solid at room temperature; they are found in meat and dairy products and palm and coconut oils. Saturated fats increase the body's own production of cholesterol.
2. Unsaturated fats are liquid at room temperature. Polyunsaturated fats are found in corn, safflower, and soybean oil. Monounsaturated fats are found in peanut and olive oils.

In addition, cholesterol, a fatty acid, is found in animal products like meat, cheese, shellfish, and eggs.

TABLE 4-1 Nutrients and Their Sources		
Nutrients	**Major Functions**	**Major Sources**
Protein	Growth, maintenance of tissue, enzymes, and hormones to regulate body processes	Meat, fish, poultry, beans, eggs, nuts, dairy products, tofu
Carbohydrates	Primary sources of energy	Bread, cereal, rice, pasta, and other grain products; fruits, vegetables, potatoes; sweets
Dietary fiber	Indigestible roughage that helps digestion	Raw barley, bulgur wheat, beans, prunes, peas, lentils, whole-grain wheat flour, oat bran. Also present in other grains, fruits, and vegetables.
Fats	Concentrated storage of energy; insulation, dissolves certain vitamins	Meats, fish, poultry, and dairy products; oils, lard, margarine; fried foods
Water	Present in all cells. Transports nutrients and wastes, takes part in many chemical reactions, cushions, regulates body temperature	All beverages. Also present to a degree in all foods.
Vitamin A	Growth, healthy skin, bones and teeth, good vision	Meat, egg yolk, dairy products, dark green leafy and deep-yellow vegetables
Thiamin (Vitamin B_1)	Helps use carbohydrates for energy, maintains healthy nervous system	Whole-grain products, enriched breads and cereals, meat, poultry, fish, beans, nuts, egg yolk
Riboflavin (Vitamin B_2)	Contributes to use of proteins, carbohydrates, and fats for energy; healthy skin	Dairy products, organ meat, green leafy vegetables, enriched breads and cereals
Niacin (Vitamin B_3)	Healthy nervous system, skin, digestion	Poultry, meat, fish, beans, nuts, dark green leafy vegetables, potatoes, whole-grain or enriched breads and cereals
Ascorbic acid (Vitamin C)	Helps hold cells together; healthy teeth, gums, and blood vessels; helps body resist infection and heal wounds	Citrus fruits and their juices, tomatoes, broccoli, raw green vegetables
Vitamin D	Needed to absorb calcium and phosphorus, healthy bones and teeth	Milk, egg yolk, liver, herring, sardines, tuna, salmon (body can make this vitamin with direct sunlight on the skin)
Vitamin E	Protects cells from oxidation (antioxidant)	Vegetable oils, margarine, wheat germ, nuts
Calcium	Needed for structure of healthy bones and teeth, healthy muscles and nerves	Dairy products, broccoli, turnips, collards, kale, mustard greens, oysters, shrimp, salmon, clams, tofu
Iodide	Prevents goiter, needed to manufacture enzyme thyroxine	Iodized salt, small amounts in seafood
Iron	Needed for healthy blood and formation of many enzymes	Liver, meat, poultry, shellfish, egg yolk, green leafy vegetables, nuts, enriched cereals and breads
Potassium	Helps in synthesis of protein, fluid balance, healthy nerves and muscles	Citrus fruits, bananas, apricots, meat, fish, and cereal
Sodium (salt)	Helps maintain fluid balance, absorb other nutrients	Table salt; processed food, especially meats and salty snacks

Source: Adapted from U.S. Department of Agriculture, *Home and Garden Bulletin No. 1*, 1978, and U.S. Department of Agriculture, Agricultural Research Service 2002, USDA National Nutrient Database for Standard Reference, Release 15. Nutrient Data Laboratory Home Page http://www.nal.usda.gov/fnic/foodcomp.

Fats and cholesterol have been the focus of much attention in recent years. Studies have linked diets high in fat, especially saturated fat and cholesterol, with increased risk of heart disease, stroke, and certain cancers, as well as with obesity. Nutritionists have been urging Americans to cut down their fat and cholesterol intake—in other words, to eat less meat, cheese, and other fatty foods—to protect their health.

There is one type of fat that most Americans don't get enough of. Omega-3, a fatty acid needed for proper brain functioning, is found in fish such as tuna, salmon, trout, and sardines. Fish also has the benefit of being low in saturated and unsaturated fats. More fish and less meat would provide a better balance and quantity of fats in the diets of most people.

Water

Water is an extremely important nutrient; it is found in every cell of the body. It transports nutrients throughout the body and removes waste products. Water cushions and lubricates parts of the body, and it is an essential part of many chemical reactions. It also helps regulate the body's temperature. Water is present in most foods, as well as in the liquids we drink. Nutritionists recommend drinking 64 ounces (eight glasses) of water a day.

Vitamins and Minerals

Protein, carbohydrates, fats, and water are the major nutrients by weight in most food. However, foods also contain trace amounts of other chemicals, called vitamins and minerals, that are essential for life and growth. Each vitamin and mineral has specific functions in the body.

Nutrients and Health

In the early 1900s, scientists discovered that many vitamins and minerals are essential to prevent certain diseases. For example, rickets, a disease that affects bone development in children, can be prevented with vitamin D and calcium, both found in fortified milk. Goiter, an enlargement of the thyroid gland, can be prevented with iodine, a mineral in iodized salt.

What Are You Eating?

Purpose: Understanding how the food you eat can impact your health is a vital component to personal health and well-being. This exercise will help you to understand the importance of watching what you eat.

Use the Food Diary page in Table 4-2 to keep track of what you eat or drink for three days. Be honest. Then review your diet. Use the information in Table 4-1 and the Nutrition Facts charts on the foods you've eaten to answer the following questions:

1. What foods were your major sources of protein?

_____

_____

_____

_____

_____

2. What foods were your major sources of carbohydrates?

_____

_____

_____

_____

_____

3. What foods were your major sources of fat?

_____

_____

_____

_____

_____

Table 4-2	Three-Day Food Diary		
Meal	**Day 1**	**Day 2**	**Day 3**
Breakfast			
Lunch			
Dinner			
Snacks			
Beverages			

4. During the three days, did you eat food that provides all the vitamins and minerals listed in Table 4-1?

_____

_____

_____

_____

If not, what vitamins and minerals did you miss?

_____

_____

_____

_____

What should you eat to make sure you get the missing vitamin(s) and mineral(s)?

_____

_____

_____

_____

5. What types of food would you like to cut down on? What types of food do you think you need to eat more of?

_____

_____

_____

_____

The relationship between diet and health in these types of disease is clear-cut. Today, nutritionists and other scientists are studying the health risks or value of other nutrients. As we've already mentioned, fat, cholesterol, and salt have been found to play a role in ailments such as high blood pressure, heart disease, and cancer. Although fat, cholesterol, and salt are not the only causes of these diseases, nutritionists recommend that people adjust their diets to reduce the risk to their health. For most Americans, a healthier diet means eating more fruits, vegetables, whole-grain products, and fish and less meat, dairy products, sweets, and salty snacks. Even young people, who may not yet be at risk for heart disease and cancer, should change their eating habits while young to prevent the development of disease in the future.

What Is a Balanced Diet?

As our understanding of nutrition has improved, the advice of nutritionists has changed. This process is continuing today. Nutritionists even disagree among themselves about what makes up a healthy diet.

Nutritionists and scientists at the U.S. Department of Agriculture and the U.S. Department of Health and Human Services periodically issue Dietary Guidelines for Americans. Their basic diet model is a high-carbohydrate diet. Their advice is threefold.

1. Aim for Fitness.
   > Aim for a healthy weight.
   > Be physically active each day.

2. Build a Healthy Base.
   > Let the Food Guide Pyramid guide your food choices (see Figure 4-1).
   > Choose a variety of grains daily, especially whole grains.
   > Choose a variety of fruits and vegetables daily.
   > Keep food safe to eat.

3. Choose Sensibly.
   > Choose a diet that is low in saturated fat and cholesterol and moderate in total fat.
   > Choose beverages and foods to moderate your intake of sugars.
   > Choose and prepare foods with less salt.
   > If you drink alcoholic beverages, do so in moderation.

To make sure you get a healthy variety of food, think of your diet in terms of the five food groups. Another way to make sure you get a balanced diet is to use the Food Guide Pyramid.

Five Food Groups

The basic five food groups are grains, vegetables, fruits, dairy products, and meats.

1. *Grains.* Whole-grain breads, cereals, tortillas, brown rice, and pasta are the healthiest of the grain products because they contain complex carbohydrates and dietary fiber. Processed grain products are white rice, muffins, waffles, sweetened cereals, doughnuts, pastry, and stuffing. These contain less fiber and sugars, salt, or fats that make them less desirable.

> Food is our common ground, a universal experience.
>
> JAMES BEARD, CHEF AND COOKBOOK AUTHOR

2. *Vegetables.* Most vegetables are extremely good for you, and you can eat as much of them as you wish. There are some exceptions, however. Canned vegetables, french fries, and pickles all contain added sugars, salt, or fats that make them less healthy choices.
3. *Fruits.* Fresh fruit is good for you, but canned fruit often contains added sugar. Dried fruit has a lot of calories.
4. *Dairy products.* Skim and 1 percent milk products and nonfat yogurt have the least fat of the dairy products. Ice milk, frozen low-fat yogurt, and 2 percent milk have moderate amounts of fat. Highest in fat are whole milk, cream and sour cream, cheeses, and ice cream. People who do not eat dairy products can find the nutrients they provide in other foods, such as meat, leafy greens, and tofu.
5. *Meat, poultry, fish, eggs, beans, and nuts.* In this group, the choices with the least fat and salt are most fish, poultry without the skin, lean cuts of beef and pork, egg whites, and beans, peas, and lentils. Oil-packed tuna, poultry with skin, most red meat, tofu, peanut butter, nuts, processed meats (cold cuts and hot dogs), and whole eggs have more fat.

The Food Guide Pyramid

The basic five food groups give you an idea of how to achieve variety in your diet. However, they do not give you a sense of how to achieve moderation as well. For that reason, in the early 1990s the USDA came up with a model of a well-balanced diet called the Food Guide Pyramid (see Figure 4-1). The pyramid is a diagram that shows the number of servings per day that should be eaten from each of the five food groups. At the base of the pyramid are foods that can be eaten in quantity—primarily grain products. As the pyramid narrows, the amount of food that should be eaten decreases, with fats and sweets at the top.

Food Guide Pyramid

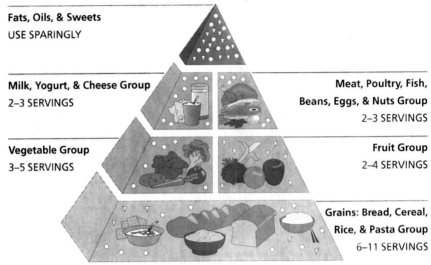

Fats, Oils, & Sweets
USE SPARINGLY

Milk, Yogurt, & Cheese Group
2–3 SERVINGS

Meat, Poultry, Fish,
Beans, Eggs, & Nuts Group
2–3 SERVINGS

Vegetable Group
3–5 SERVINGS

Fruit Group
2–4 SERVINGS

Grains: Bread, Cereal,
Rice, & Pasta Group
6–11 SERVINGS

Figure 4-1: The USDA Food Guide Pyramid shows how much to eat from each of the food groups. The bigger the section of the pyramid, the more of that food group should be eaten. As you can see, this is a high-carbohydrate diet. Grains make up much more of the pyramid than the other food groups do.

Source: U.S. Department of Agriculture and U.S. Department of Health and Human Services, *Dietary Guidelines for Americans,* 2000, p. 15.

The number of servings recommended by the USDA depends on your age, sex, size, and level of activity:

> Children age two to six, inactive women, and some older adults require the fewest servings per day of each group, about 1,600 calories total.
> Older children, teenage girls, active women, and most men require an average number of servings per day from each group, about 2,200 calories total.
> Teenage boys and active men need the maximum number of servings per day, about 2,800 calories total.

Changing Your Eating Habits

If your diet is less than satisfactory, you can change it. The first step is to keep a food diary of what you eat for a few days. Once you've done that, you can analyze your eating habits and decide what changes are necessary.

In addition to reviewing what you eat to see whether your diet has an adequate variety of foods, you can also compare the quantities you eat with the recommendations shown on the Food Guide Pyramid. The serving sizes on the food pyramid are often smaller than those found on Nutrition Facts charts or than typical portion sizes. For example, one slice of bread equals one serving of grain. That means a sandwich has two servings of grain.

If you are like most Americans, you will find you need to cut down on fats, sweets, and processed grains and eat more whole grains, fruits, and vegetables.

After you've thought about what you eat and how much you eat, you should also consider your eating habits. For example, do you skip breakfast? That's a bad habit, because breakfast fuels the start of your day and helps spread your eating into smaller meals. Studies have shown that eating several small meals each day rather than one or two large meals helps prevent the storage of fat. Last, consider your weight. If you have a healthy weight, changing your eating habits may simply mean adjusting your diet so it has a better balance of foods

News & Views

The Other Food Guide Pyramids

When the Food Guide Pyramid came out, many Americans looked at it and asked, "Where is the food I eat?" Ethnic Americans wondered where were tortillas, grits, cornbread, couscous, guava, and other foods they loved. Lactose-intolerant Americans, who cannot digest milk products, wondered what to do about the dairy products group. And vegetarians knew the pyramid didn't fit their diet at all.

The U.S. Department of Agriculture (USDA) heard these points, but they maintained that the pyramid is just a general guide based on the meat- and dairy-based diet most Americans eat. So nutritionists around the country began adapting the pyramid to the cuisines of different ethnic and special groups.

> The Soul Food Pyramid, based on the traditional African American diet, added grits and cornbread to the grains group, black-eyed peas to the meats group, and chitterlings to the fats, oils, and sweets group.
> The Asian Diet Pyramid, based on Chinese and other East Asian cuisines, added millet to the grains group and moved meat all the way to the top.
> The Mexican Food Pyramid added lard and avocados to the fats, oils, and sweets group, salsa and chilies to the vegetable group, and tortillas to the grain group.
> The Mediterranean Diet Pyramid, based on Italian, Spanish, Greek, and other Mediterranean cuisines, added polenta and couscous to the grains group and moved olive oil from the top to right above fruits and vegetables.

And these are just a few of the pyramids that have been developed since the USDA pyramid was published. Others pyramids are based on Arab, Chinese, Cuban, Indian, Italian, Japanese, Native American, Portuguese, Russian, Spanish, Thai, and vegetarian diets. Even though the USDA does not endorse these special pyramids, they do provide a Web page with links to all of them. Visit the Food and Nutrition Information Center of the USDA Web site to check them out: http://www.nal.usda.gov/fnic/etext.

Source: "Ethnic/Cultural and Special Audience Food Guide Pyramids," U.S. Department of Agriculture, Food and Nutrition Information Center, http://www.nal.usda./gov/fnic/, accessed February 6, 2003; Jenny Deam, "Rebuilding the Food Pyramid: Critics Charge USDA's Guides Fail Ethnic Test," *Denver Post,* July 25, 2000, pp. 1E, 8E.

Healthy Weights

Eat to live, and not live to eat.

BENJAMIN FRANKLIN,
18TH-CENTURY
STATESMAN,
SCIENTIST,
AND WRITER

More than half of Americans are overweight or obese. Being overweight or underweight is not simply an appearance issue. It's a health issue. Overweight people have a higher risk of developing high blood pressure, heart disease, stroke, certain types of diabetes, and some cancers. Underweight people have a higher risk of health problems as well. Underweight women have a greater chance of developing osteoporosis, a bone disease, and underweight men and women, on average, do not live as long as people whose weight is healthy.

Finding Out Your Body Mass Index

Is your weight healthy? Your body mass index (BMI) will tell you. BMI is a measure of weight in relation to height. In the BMI chart shown in Figure 4-2, find your weight along the horizontal axis. Go straight up from that point to the line that matches your height. Then look to see which BMI group you fall into.

> When you enjoy what you do, you never get tired.
>
> DONALD TRUMP, REAL ESTATE DEVELOPER

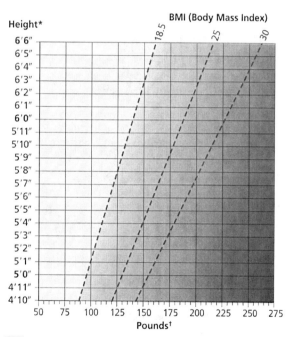

Figure 4-2: This chart shows the BMI ranges for healthy, overweight, and obese people. A healthy BMI ranges from 18.5 to 25.

Source: U.S. Department of Agriculture and U.S. Department of Health and Human Services, *Dietary Guidelines for Americans,* 2000, p. 7.

Healthy Weight BMI from 18.5 up to 25 refers to healthy weight.

Overweight BMI from 25 up to 30 refers to overweight.

Obese BMI 30 or higher refers to obesity. Obese persons are also overweight.

*Without shoes

†Without clothes

Exercise

Modern life, with cars, office work, computers, and TV, tends to make couch potatoes of us all. For most of us, physical activity is not a natural part of the daily routine. To be active, we must make a conscious decision to exercise or play sports.

People who exercise regularly look better because they have more muscle than fat. They are stronger, more energetic, and more flexible. And perhaps most important, people who are fit feel better about themselves, both physically and mentally.

Becoming Fit

What is physical fitness? The President's Council on Physical Fitness and Sports suggests that physical fitness is the ability to carry out daily tasks without tiring and with enough energy left to enjoy leisure activities and to handle an emergency requiring physical exertion. Your own level of fitness is determined to a great extent by your daily routine—your work or schooling, your sports activities, and how much you walk in the course of the day. To improve your normal level of fitness, you must add exercise or sports to your regular routine.

A person who is truly physically fit has good

> cardiorespiratory endurance—the ability to do moderately strenuous activity over a period of time without overtaxing the heart and lungs.
> muscular strength—the ability to exert force in a single try.
> muscular endurance—the ability to repeat movements or to hold a position for a long time without tiring.
> flexibility—the ability to move a joint through its full range of motion.
> body composition—the proportion of the body made of muscle compared with fat.

Different types of physical activities improve different aspects of fitness. In general, aerobic activities such as running, basketball, step training, and tennis are best for cardiorespiratory endurance and body composition. Activities such as calisthenics, weight training, karate, yoga, and stretching improve strength, endurance, and flexibility.

Rate Your Level of Activity

Purpose: You can check your level of physical activity by rating how hard, how long, and how often you exercise. This exercise will help you to rate your own fitness level.

Circle your score for each question.

1. How hard do you exercise in a typical session?

	Score
no change in pulse	0
little change in heart rate (slow walking, bowling, yoga)	1
small increase in heart rate and breathing (table tennis, active golf)	2
moderate increase in heart rate and breathing (rapid walking, dancing, easy swimming)	3
occasional heavy breathing and sweating (tennis, basketball, squash)	4
sustained heavy breathing and sweating (jogging, aerobic dance)	5

2. How long do you exercise at one session?

	Score
less than 5 minutes	0
5 to 14 minutes	1
15 to 29 minutes	2
30 to 44 minutes	3
45 to 59 minutes	4
60 minutes or more	5

3. How often do you exercise?

	Score
less than once a week	0
once a week	1
2 times a week	2
3 times a week	3
4 times a week	4
5 or more times a week	5

4. Now take your scores from each question above and multiply them. Rate your activity level as follows:

Score	Activity Level
less than 15	inactive
15–24	somewhat active
25–40	moderately active
41–60	active
over 60	very active

If your score is 41 or higher, you are active enough to enjoy a wide variety of physical activities. If your score is less than 41, you should approach a change in your physical fitness program gradually and with caution. Anyone who is starting a new or increased physical fitness program should check with his or her doctor first.

Sticking to an Exercise Program

Many people start an exercise program with the best intentions, and within several months they quit. To avoid this fate and to make physical activity part of your routine, follow these guidelines:

> Choose a friend or relative, and make an agreement with them to exercise. Be sure to write it down.

> Be specific. Write down the days you will exercise, what you will do, and the number of months you will do it.

> Include rewards and punishments. Specify what you'll do to earn a reward and what will result in punishment—doing an unpleasant chore, for example.

> Get the person with whom you made the agreement to support you. This will make it harder to skip sessions or quit.

Rest

Eating well and exercising are two components of maintaining good health. A third essential component is adequate rest. More than a hundred years ago, Thomas Edison invented the lightbulb and radically changed people's sleeping habits. Whereas people used to sleep at night because doing anything else was impractical, now it's possible to ignore the body's natural rhythms and stay awake. The result? We sometimes get less rest than we need.

Scientists have found that our bodies operate according to circadian rhythms, an inner time clock that roughly matches the 24-hour cycle of night and day. People with irregular schedules often suffer from sleep problems. Airline pilots, for example, who work long shifts and cross time zones, often suffer fatigue. People whose sleep is irregular tend to be fatigued, less efficient, and irritable.

To feel good and perform at your peak, regular sleep habits are essential. If you are a poor sleeper, consider these suggestions to improve your sleep habits:

> Follow a regular schedule for sleeping and waking up, even on weekends.
> Exercise regularly.
> Don't eat or drink anything with caffeine after midday. Caffeine, a stimulant found in coffee, tea, chocolate, and cola drinks, can keep you awake.
> Before bedtime, do whatever relaxes you. Read, watch TV, listen to music, or take a hot bath.
> Avoid alcoholic beverages before bed. They may help you fall asleep, but they interfere with your staying asleep.
> Don't worry about not sleeping. If you can't sleep, get up and do something boring until you feel sleepy.

> He who has health, has hope; and he who has hope, has everything.
>
> ARABIAN PROVERB

> The sleep of a laboring man is sweet.
>
> ECCLESIASTES, A BOOK OF THE BIBLE

Drug Abuse

In this unit, we've discussed things that help maintain your health: good food, exercise, and rest, all of which contribute to your physical and mental well-being. Unfortunately,

> I never take a nap after dinner but when I have had a bad night, and then the nap takes me.
>
> SAMUEL JOHNSON, 18TH-CENTURY ENGLISH AUTHOR

many Americans also use drugs, which are chemical substances that create a physical, mental, emotional, or behavioral change in the user. Some drugs, of course, are used properly as prescription medicines under the care of a doctor. But others, such as alcohol, nicotine, and cocaine, are misused.

Nicotine

Cigarettes, cigars, and other forms of tobacco contain nicotine, a stimulant. A stimulant is a drug that increases brain activity and other body functions. Stimulants (like nicotine and caffeine) make the user feel more awake. Nicotine stimulates the heart and nervous system, raising blood pressure and making the heart beat faster.

The life expectancy of smokers is shorter than that of nonsmokers. On average, women who smoke live 14.5 fewer years than women who don't smoke. Men who smoke live 13 fewer years than men who don't smoke. Smoking is the major cause of death from cancer of the lungs, throat, and mouth. It contributes to heart disease and respiratory problems. According to the Centers for Disease Control and Prevention, about 440,000 Americans die from smoking-related causes each year.

Alcohol

One of the most abused drugs in the United States is alcohol. Almost 8 percent of American adults characterize themselves as heavy drinkers. More than 30 percent admit to binge drinking. Alcohol is a depressant, a drug that decreases brain activity and raises blood pressure. Large amounts of alcohol dull sensation and harm judgment, memory, and coordination, eventually causing unconsciousness and sometimes death.

Alcohol becomes a problem when it interferes with a person's functioning in school, on the job, or in relationships. Heavy alcohol use is associated with other problems: death and injury from drunk driving, sexual assaults, unplanned and unsafe sex, academic failure, and vandalism.

The Dragon Slayers

If you break a bone near Aniak, Alaska, don't be surprised if the EMTs who come to your rescue are teenaged girls. In Aniak, a village 320 miles west of Anchorage, teenagers serve as the community's emergency medical team, the Dragon Slayers.

The Dragon Slayers were formed in 1993 by Pete Brown, the volunteer fire chief of Aniak. Brown didn't have any adults available to respond to daytime emergency calls, so he got his daughter Mariah and several other teens to help. The first group of Dragon Slayers were mostly children of firefighters, and most were boys. But as time went on, the boys preferred hunting and snowboarding to attending the Tuesday night training meetings. The group eventually became an all-girl team.

To join the Dragon Slayers, local teens must be passing their high school courses. They also must complete emergency trauma training, the American Red Cross advanced first aid course, and the American Heart Association's CPR training.

The teenagers wear beepers, and even their teachers at school have learned to let them go gracefully when the beeper goes off. Some calls are close by; in 2000 they saved the life of the school principal, a diabetic. But many calls are

COURTESY OF ANIAK HIGH SCHOOL, ANIAK, ALASKA

distant, since the Aniak volunteers serve a rural area the size of Maryland. Traveling by snowmobile, four-wheel drive vehicles, and boat, the teens respond to 450 calls a year. They have set bones, resuscitated heart attack victims, rescued injured snowmobilers, and delivered babies.

With their experience, it's no surprise that many of the first Dragon Slayers are training for related careers. Mariah Brown joined the Navy to become a rescue swimmer. Another is taking medical courses on line and hopes to become a doctor. A third is a flight paramedic. And one Dragon Slayer has stayed in Aniak and become an adult volunteer firefighter. As the Dragon Slayers grow up and move on, another group is behind them—the Lizard Killers, preteens in EMT training.

Source: Dina Blair, "Snow Angels," WGN TV, November 10, 2002 http://wgntv.trb.com/templates/misc/printstory.jsp?slug=wgntv%2D111002medicalwatch, accessed February 14, 2003; Christina Cheakalos and Lyndon Stambler, "Snow Angels," People, June 3, 2002; Danielle Wolffe, "Young Women Meet Emergency Services Need in Aniak," Kenai Peninsula Online, September 30, 2001, http://peninsulaclarion.com/stories/093001/ala_093001ala0140001.shtml, accessed January 16, 2003.

Other Drugs

When you take illegal drugs, your exposure to risk increases. First, you don't know what you're actually buying when you buy drugs on the street. Second, you are subject to arrest for possession of illegal substances. And third, the long-term effects of some drugs are still unknown. Some of the more common abused drugs are briefly discussed here.

Marijuana

Marijuana slows thinking and reaction time, distorts perceptions, and upsets balance and coordination. Its use creates mild feelings of pleasure. Marijuana has many negative effects. Like alcohol, it harms the coordination and reaction time needed to drive a car or operate machinery. Marijuana interferes with the process of forming memories, an effect that continues beyond the period of smoking. Therefore, using marijuana interferes with a person's ability to learn.

Amphetamines

Amphetamines, known popularly as "uppers" or "speed," are stimulants. They help people stay awake and gather energy for tasks. Abuse of amphetamines can cause weight loss, malnutrition, pain, and unconsciousness. Heavy users are prone to violence and aggression.

Barbiturates and Benzodiazepines

Barbiturates (barbs, reds, and yellows) and benzodiazepines (tranquilizers, tranks, downers, sleeping pills, Valium) are depressants. They slow the activity of the nervous and cardiovascular systems, making people calm down and feel relaxed and sleepy. Different types of barbiturates and benzodiazepines create different levels of physical and psychological dependence. Users who stop taking them experience tremors, nausea, cramps, and vomiting.

Club Drugs

The term *club drugs* refers to a wide variety of drugs used by young adults at parties, dance clubs, raves, and bars. The most common club drugs are MDMA (ecstasy, X); GHB (G, Georgia home boy); Rohypnol (forget-me pill, roofies); ketamine (K, special K, vitamin K); and methamphetamine (chalk, ice, meth). These drugs have a variety of effects, which are summarized in Table 4-3. The club drugs are even more harmful when taken in combination with alcohol.

Some club drugs are colorless, odorless, and tasteless. They can easily be slipped into a drink in order to intoxicate or sedate other people. In recent years there have been reports of club drugs being used to commit sexual assaults.

> The basic thing nobody asks is, why do people take drugs of any sort?
>
> JOHN LENNON,
> ONE OF THE BEATLES

Cocaine

Cocaine, a stimulant, acts on the brain to produce a brief rush of happiness and excitement. As the dose wears off, feelings of panic, depression, and anxiety set in. Cocaine can be sniffed, injected, or smoked. Crack, a powerful form of cocaine, is smoked, so it enters the bloodstream quickly and in higher concentrations. Since it is difficult to estimate a dose of crack, users sometimes overdose, suffering convulsions, cardiac arrest, coma, and death.

The long-term use of cocaine often leads to emotional disturbances, paranoia, fear, nervousness, insomnia, and weight loss. Many people become unable to function normally at work or with their families. Their lives are focused on getting and using the drug.

Steroids

Anabolic steroid is a synthetic form of the male hormone, testosterone. Because the drug increases the body's ability to turn protein into muscle, steroids are popular among athletes and others who wish to improve their athletic performance and appearance.

Table 4-3   The Most Common Club Drugs

Drug	Form	Short-Term Effects	Potential Health Effects
MDMA *Ecstasy, XTC, Adam, clarity, lover's speed*	Tablet or capsule	• Stimulant: increased heart rate, blood pressure; feelings of alertness and energy; mild hallucinogenic effects • In high doses, can lead to high body temperature, dehydration, and death	Depression, sleep problems, anxiety, impaired memory and learning
GHB *Grievous bodily harm, G, liquid ecstasy, Georgia home boy*	• Clear liquid, white powder, tablet, or capsule • Often made in home laboratories	• Depressant: reduced heart rate, blood pressure; reduced pain and anxiety; feeling of relaxation and well-being; reduced inhibitions • In high doses, can lead to drowsiness, loss of consciousness, coma, and death • Has been used in sexual assaults	Unknown
Ketamine *Special K, K, vitamin K, cat Valiums*	• Liquid for injection, powder for snorting or smoking • Used legally as an anesthetic, usually for animals	• Increased heart rate and blood pressure; poor coordination • In high doses, can cause delirium, amnesia, depression, respiratory problems, and death	Memory loss; numbness; nausea and vomiting
Rohypnol *Roofies, rophies, roche, forget-me pill*	• Pill • Used legally in Europe as a sleeping pill	• Depressant: reduced heart rate, blood pressure; reduced pain and anxiety; feeling of relaxation and well-being; reduced inhibitions • Visual and digestive disturbances; urine retention • Has been used in sexual assaults	Loss of memory for period while under the effects of the drug
Methamphetamine *Speed, ice, chalk, meth, crystal, crank, fire, glass*	Many forms; can be smoked, snorted, injected, or taken orally	• Stimulant: increased heart rate, blood pressure; feelings of alertness and energy • Agitation, excited speech, decreased appetite, aggression, violence, and psychotic behavior	Memory loss, heart damage, nervous system damage

Experts say that steroid users face side effects and risks that are not fully understood. Women risk changes in their sexual characteristics, including shrinking of the breasts, growth of body hair, baldness, and a deepened voice. Some men suffer high blood pressure, lowered sperm counts, and acute acne. In addition, steroids seem to be as addictive as alcohol or nicotine.

Heroin

Heroin is a depressant that makes its user feel happy, safe, and peaceful. It is physically addictive, and users need greater amounts of it as they become tolerant of its effects.

When users stop taking heroin, they experience agonizing symptoms including nausea, shaking, chills, vomiting, and pain. Stopping the psychological dependence on heroin is even more difficult, because addicts have poor self-belief and rely on the drug to escape from reality.

ELEMENTS OF EXCELLENCE

After reading this chapter, you have learned

> how the interplay of your health, your lifestyle, and your nutrition choices impact your potential.
> what an active lifestyle can mean to your emotional and physical well-being.
> how stress, rest, and sleep can impact your health and ability to function effectively.
> the pitfalls of drug use and abuse and their impact on your ability to function at your best.

The Information Highway

Getting Up to Speed

There are many Web sites and discussion groups about health issues:

> Government advice on healthy eating can be found on the Food and Nutrition Information Center of the U.S. Department of Agriculture Web site. You can download several publications, including the Dietary Guidelines for Americans, which includes the Food Guide Pyramid. You can also click on links to other food and nutrition resources on the Web: **http://www.nal.usda.gov**.
> The American Dietetic Association provides lots of information on food and nutrition, plus links to other nutrition sites: **http://www.eat right.org**.
> The President's Council on Physical Fitness and Sports provides information and advice about exercise, weight control, and fitness for disabled and older people: **http://www.fitness.gov**.

> The Substance Abuse and Mental Health Services Administration, a part of the U.S. Department of Health and Human Services, provides information on the treatment and prevention of various types of substance abuse: **http://www.samhsa.gov**.

> The HealthScout Network is a commercial consumer health site with personalized health management tools. These include health alerts, newsletters, mini-checkups, and family health pages: **http://www. healthscout.com**.

In addition, you can use a search engine to find information about nutrition, the Food Guide Pyramid, dietary guidelines, body mass index, specific types of exercise and sports; sleep; alcohol, tobacco, and other specific drugs; and other health issues.

JOURNAL

Answer the following journal questions.

1. What does food mean to you and your family? What foods reflect your family's heritage?

_____

_____

_____

_____

_____

_____

_____

_____

_____

_____

_____

_____

2. What changes do you plan to make to your diet after reading this chapter?

_____

_____

_____

_____

_____

_____

_____

_____

_____

_____

_____

3. What sport or type of exercise do you enjoy the most? What fitness benefits do you gain as a result of this activity?

_____

_____

_____

_____

_____

_____

_____

_____

_____

_____

_____

4. Describe someone you know who abuses drugs. What problems does this person—and the people around him or her—have as a result? What approach might help this person get off drugs?

_____

_____

_____

_____

_____

_____

_____

_____

_____

_____

_____

5. Describe your ideal of perfect fitness and health.

_____

_____

_____

_____

_____

_____

_____

_____

_____

_____

_____

Chapter 5

Communicating Effectively

At six months, a baby cries, laughs, smiles, makes faces, and waves its arms and legs to communicate. Although strangers may not know what the baby is trying to say, the parents probably do. By 18 months, babies speak a few words and can change their tone of voice to reflect their moods. Still, people who don't know the baby well can't understand much of what the baby's trying to communicate. Frustration often results because the baby can't get the people close by to respond properly. As babies grow into children, they acquire more communication skills. They speak, listen, write, and read, and the quality of their communication improves. As children mature and become adults, they become even more effective communicators, and their ability to get along with others, as well as their own sense of well-being, improves.

Although most of us take communication for granted, its importance cannot be overestimated. Good communication is the basis of our social potential. Without it, each of us would live dreary lives in isolation. It's no accident that solitary confinement is one of the harshest punishments. We need other people, and our connections to others are forged by communication. This chapter will explore this important connection.

APWIDE WORLD PHOTOS/RON EDMONDS

Trained as an actor, President Ronald Reagan used clear, simple language and spoke in a relaxed and direct manner. He communicated so effectively with the American people that he earned the nickname "the Great Communicator."

What Is Communication?

Communication is the exchange of messages. Messages can be verbal, using spoken or written words, or they can be nonverbal, using symbols, gestures, expressions, and body language. For communication to take place, there must be a sender, a person who transmits the message. There must also be a receiver, a person who receives the message. Effective communication occurs when the sender and the receiver have the same understanding of the message (see Figure 5-1).

One-Way and Two-Way Communication

There are two basic patterns for the communication process. The first is one-way communication, and the second is two-way communication.

In one-way communication, the sender transmits a message, the receiver gets it, and the process is complete. When a mail order house sends you a catalog, and you look at it and throw it away, one-way communication has taken place. Another example of one-way communication occurs when your instructor tells you the next assignment and you write it down and leave the classroom.

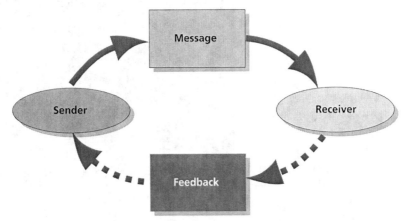

Figure 5-1: The communication process: The sender transmits a message, the receiver gets the message, and the receiver sends another message—the feedback—to the sender, and the process starts again.

In two-way communication, the sender transmits a message, the receiver gets it, and the receiver responds with another message. Sender and receiver alternate roles, giving one another feedback. Conversations and correspondence are examples of two-way communication.

One-way communication has the advantage of being fast. It also maintains the speaker's authority, since no feedback—either negative or positive—is expected of the listener. For example, in the armed forces, one-way communication is used to transmit orders and maintain the authority of rank. But one-way communication is far less effective than two-way communication. In one-way communication, the speaker has no way of determining whether the receiver has received the correct message, because there is no feedback. In contrast, two-way communication provides an opportunity for both parties to correct mistakes and misunderstandings.

Both one-way and two-way communication can take place in many types of situations and between different types of senders and receivers. Both patterns can take place between two people, between one person and a small group, between one person and a large group, and even between groups. Table 5-1 shows examples of one-way and two-way communication between different types of senders and receivers.

Nonverbal Communication

Most people think of words as the chief means by which we communicate. Being clear, concise, and courteous in your choice of words is important. However, studies of face-to-face communication have shown that 80 to 90 percent of the impact of a message comes from nonverbal elements—facial expressions, eye contact, body language, and tone of voice. Nonverbal communication can be far more revealing of the content of a message than its words. The speaker usually has more control over choice of words than over facial expressions, eye contact, body language, and tone of voice. The expression, "It wasn't what he said, it was how he said it" reflects this truth. Words may say one thing while the body communicates another message.

> The face [is] the index of a feeling mind.
>
> GEORGE CRABBE,
> 18TH–19TH CENTURY
> ENGLISH POET

Nonverbal communication varies from culture to culture, as the News & Views on page 87 describes. Because the United States is a multicultural society, it's important to be sensitive to cultural differences in communication. Sometimes it may be necessary to alter interactions with others based on the perception of cultural differences in nonverbal communication.

TABLE 5–1   Examples of One-Way and Two-Way Communication

Sender and Receiver	Example of One-Way Communication	Example of Two-Way Communication
Two individuals	An employer dictates a letter to her assistant.	Employer and assistant discuss a business problem.
An individual and a small group	A teacher sends a change-of-address e-mail message to all his e-mail correspondents.	A teacher leads a discussion in a small class.
An individual and a large group	The president of the United States delivers the State of the Union address to all U.S. citizens (and the world).	The president of the United States has a press conference with news-paper, magazine, and broadcast journalists.
A group and an individual	The Internal Revenue Service sends a tax refund check to a taxpayer.	The Internal Revenue Service notifies a taxpayer that she must respond to a question about unreported income.
Two groups	A student group puts posters advertising a rock concert all over campus.	A student group negotiates an agreement with a rock group to perform on campus.

Facial Expressions

Smiling, frowning, and raising your eyebrows are just a few of the thousands of movements of which your face is capable. These movements communicate feelings. Researchers have found that many facial expressions are universal. A frown means the same thing in Detroit as it does in Bombay. The intensity and frequency of facial expressions vary from culture to culture.

Misperception of Nonverbal Communication

Most people are good at judging a speaker's feelings from his or her expressions. Sadness, anger, hostility, excitement, and happiness are easily conveyed by expressions. But people are less accurate when it comes to judging character from facial expressions. For example, many people think that a person who nods and smiles a lot is warm and agreeable, but studies have shown no such correlation. People of differing cultures also have unique forms of nonverbal communication, and oftentimes, assumptions are made that are inaccurate. Be sure to "see" each person for their whole person, and realize that every person shows their emotions differently.

News & Views

Gestures: One Culture's "Good Luck" Is Another Culture's Insult

Some gestures do not need words to have meaning. Gestures such as a salute and a shake of the head have meaning without words. Each culture has its own gestures that people use to communicate. However, sometimes the same gesture has different meanings in different cultures. When that happens, people from different cultures can unintentionally confuse or offend one another.

In most parts of the world, for example, "victory" is conveyed by an upraised palm with the second and third fingers in a V-shape. If you make that gesture in Great Britain, however, you will be giving someone a sexual insult (similar in meaning to the middle-finger upward jerk of the United States).

The thumbs-up gesture means that all is well in much of Europe and North America. But in Greece and Turkey, the thumbs-up sign is a sexual insult. Another insult in Greece and Turkey is called the hand of Moutza. It is an open palm with the fingers extended, held facing the person being insulted. The origin of the palm of Moutza goes back 1,500 years. At that time ordinary citizens helped punish prisoners by pressing handfuls of dung into their faces. So be careful not to signal "five things" using your hand when in Greece or Turkey!

Another gesture that can cause misunderstanding is the sign of the University of Texas football team, the Longhorns. At a college football game, extending the second finger and the pinkie is a sign of encouragement and victory to the Longhorns. However, the same gesture in Italy and other parts of Europe means that a man's wife has been unfaithful—a terrible insult.

Similarly, crossing your fingers means luck in the United States. But in some Asian countries, crossing your fingers means you are making a sexual offer.

So be aware when you are communicating with people from another culture. The gestures whose meanings you take for granted may not mean what you think they mean to a person from another culture.

Source: Peter Marsh, Ed., *Eye to Eye: How People Interact,* Topsfield, MA: Salem House, 1988, p. 54; Carole Wade and Carol Tavris, *Psychology,* 4th ed, New York: HarperCollins, 1996, p. 670.

Eye Contact

Smiles and frowns may have a common meaning throughout the world, but eye contact does not. In some cultures, looking downward while speaking to someone is a sign of respect. In mainstream U.S. culture, however, a person who doesn't meet your eyes during conversation is thought to be hiding something. Making eye contact with someone when speaking to them is considered desirable in the United States.

In mainstream American culture, eye contact is used to establish communication. For example, if you want salespeople to help you, you try to make eye contact with them. If you don't want your instructors to call on you in class, you avoid their eyes in the hope that they will not notice you.

> If his lips are silent, he chatters with his fingertips; betrayal oozes out of him at every pore.
>
> SIGMUND FREUD,
> AUSTRIAN FOUNDER
> OF PSYCHOANALYSIS

Body Language

Try to speak for two minutes and hold your head, arms, and legs completely still. Impossible? Probably. Without being aware of it, people move their bodies constantly while they talk. They nod, shrug, gesture with their hands, and shift their weight. Body language can indicate a wide range of emotion from boredom (yawning) to impatience (tapping your fingers or feet) to enthusiasm (gesturing with your hands).

In addition to communicating meaning by moving the body, people communicate by the distance they leave between themselves. In mainstream U.S. culture, people who are lovers, close family members, or intimate friends are comfortable standing about a foot apart. Acquaintances or colleagues, on the other hand, usually stand 4 to 12 feet apart when communicating. The tone of an interaction can be changed just by changing the distance between two people.

Culture and Body Language

The meaning of body language and distance varies from one culture to another. In some cultures, gestures are expansive and expressive. In other cultures, body language is controlled to avoid showing too much emotion. Each culture has extensive unwritten rules about body language. For example, if a stranger walked up to you and stopped one foot away, you would feel threatened. That's because a person you don't know has entered space that's reserved for people you know intimately.

Voice Qualities

A voice can be loud or soft, high or low pitched, fast or slow. Its tone can be pleasant, harsh, or monotonous. Voice qualities can convey whether you are interested, bored, tired, or happy.

It's sometimes risky to make generalizations about what voice qualities mean. For example, a New Yorker may speak faster than someone from Atlanta. When they speak to one another, the New Yorker may feel the Southerner is slow to understand and the Southerner may perceive the New Yorker as rude. Neither one of them would necessarily be right. On the other hand, people who know one another well are very good at picking up meaningful changes in voice quality. You probably have had the experience of knowing that something was bothering a friend because of the tone of voice you heard.

> I do not much dislike the matter, but the manner of his speech.
>
> WILLIAM SHAKESPEARE,
> 16TH–17TH CENTURY
> ENGLISH DRAMATIST
> AND POET

Barriers to Communication

Effective communication means that both sender and receiver have the same understanding of the message. The first prerequisite is that the message, both verbal and nonverbal, should be clear. But beyond the message itself are factors that influence both the sender and the receiver. Each person brings a distinct set of abilities, knowledge, experience, attitudes, and feelings to the communication process. Miscommunication may occur because of physical, mental, or emotional barriers on the part of the communicators.

Observing Nonverbal Communication

Purpose: Here's an activity that will improve your awareness of nonverbal communication. Observe a conversation at a supermarket or mall. Pay particular attention to nonverbal communication. Write what you observed in the space provided.

1. What facial expressions did you notice?

_____

_____

_____

_____

_____

2. Did the people maintain eye contact throughout the conversation? If not, when was eye contact broken?

_____

_____

_____

_____

_____

3. What body postures, head movements, and gestures did they use?

_____

_____

_____

_____

_____

4. Describe the voices.

Volume _____

Pitch _____

Speed _____

Tone _____

When you communicate, you can take responsibility for your share of the process. You can try to overcome barriers to communication by making the message you send clear. If you receive a negative or unexpected response, examine yourself first to see if your message is the cause. You may have to overcome communication barriers by revising your message.

Physical Barriers

Any disturbing factor in the physical environment or your body can prevent full communication. If the room is noisy, you may not be able to hear or make yourself heard. If there is a lot of other activity, you may find yourself distracted. If you are sitting or standing in an awkward position, your discomfort may act as a barrier to communication. In some cases, hearing loss makes it difficult to understand what's being communicated.

Mental Barriers

Every person has a unique set of knowledge and experience that influences what he or she does. When you communicate, for example, you tend to interpret what's being said in light of your previous knowledge and experience. People make assumptions all the time, and frequently they are wrong.

Another type of mental barrier that prevents good communication is selective attention. People tend to focus on what interests them and pay little or no attention to the rest. Or we pay attention to positive matters and ignore unpleasant ones. During a performance evaluation, for example, an employee may remember each word of praise, while his boss's criticisms don't even register!

Another mental barrier to good communication is choice of words. In some cases, communication breaks down because one of the people involved simply doesn't understand the vocabulary of the other. When someone uses technical, specialized words to explain how a machine works, for example, a nontechnical person may not understand. Or communication may break down because one person "talks down" to another, and the second person becomes resentful. In other cases, the words being used are emotionally charged. Discussions about politics, for example, frequently go nowhere because people have long-standing emotional associations with words such as *conservative, liberal, left, right, Republican,* and *Democrat.*

> Hating people because of their color is wrong, and it doesn't matter which color does the hating. It's just plain wrong.
>
> MUHAMMAD ALI,
> BOXING CHAMPION

Emotional Barriers

Feelings and emotions can also create barriers to communication. Stress, fear, happiness, anger, and love can all prevent effective communication. A person who is worried about something, for example, finds it hard to pay attention during an important meeting.

People's long-held feelings and attitudes can also cause communication problems. Prejudice, which is a negative attitude toward people because of their membership in a group, is a communication barrier. It prevents people from communicating effectively as individuals because their attitudes can cloud the sending and receiving of messages.

Lack of Rapport

The physical, mental, and emotional barriers to communication all have the same basic effect: They drive a wedge between the two communicators. In essence, the two communicators lack rapport, or harmony. This situation is so common that there are several expressions to describe it: "They're not on the same wavelength," "They're out of sync," "There's no chemistry between them," and "They're two ships that pass in the night."

Without rapport, people who try to communicate have a difficult time. Misunderstandings, hard feelings, and mistakes are the consequences. How can you establish rapport and communicate effectively? We'll try to answer that question in the rest of this chapter.

Communication Styles

The key to effective communication is awareness—of yourself but, more important, of the people with whom you communicate. You must be conscious of the feelings, needs, and personalities of the people around you. Once you become sensitive to others, you will find that their response to you is more positive. Naturally, both people and the communication process are extremely complex. No two people or communication situations are alike.

The work of David Merrill and Roger Reid proposed that people show two major forms of behavior when they communicate: responsiveness and assertiveness. Responsiveness is the degree to which people are closed or open in their dealings with others. Those who have a low degree of responsiveness hide emotion and are very self-controlled. On the other hand, people who have a high degree of responsiveness show emotion and seem friendly. Reid defines assertiveness as behavior ranging from asking questions (low assertiveness) to telling others what's expected (high assertiveness).

News & Views

E-Mail Etiquette

In the past, you might have written a letter, made a phone call, or typed a memo. Today you are more likely to communicate with friends, family, and coworkers by e-mail. E-mail is so fast and convenient that people often dash off messages without much thought or care. The result can be ineffective communication or, worse, miscommunication.

Writing an E-Mail Message

Here are some pointers for writing effective e-mail:

> Use an informative subject line. That way the recipient can easily see the topic of your message.
> Start your message with a salutation (Dear Mr. Brenner or Hi Mom), just as you would a written or typed letter.

- Keep your message short and to the point. People don't like to do lots of reading on a computer.
- Don't write anything you wouldn't want the whole world to see, because e-mail is not private. Your recipient may decide to forward your message to a large group of people. In addition, many companies routinely review and save employee e-mails, whether business or personal.
- DON'T USE ALL CAPITAL LETTERS BECAUSE THEY ARE HARD TO READ. THEY ARE ALSO CONSIDERED BAD MANNERS, LIKE SHOUTING.
- Don't write "flame" e-mails, messages that are insulting and meant to hurt. Wait until you cool down to send any e-mail message.
- As a courtesy, put your name at the end of your message. To make this easier, create signature blocks you can insert automatically.
- Check and proofread your message. Use a spell-check tool as well.

Sending E-Mail

Once your message is written and checked, think about the transmission options before you hit any keys.

- Send CC copies of the message only to those who really need to see it. (The abbreviation CC means "carbon copy" and dates back to typewriter days.)
- Use BCC copies when you are sending a message to a group of people who don't know one another and who might not want their e-mail addresses seen by strangers. (BCC means "blind carbon copy.") With BCC copies, recipients see only their own e-mail address and yours.
- Don't spam—send impersonal e-mail messages to large groups.

Using Smilies

When you talk to someone face to face, you see the other person's facial expression and gestures. These supplement the message in the words. E-mail users have a group of keyboard symbols that add visual cues to e-mail messages. Called smilies, they usually appear at the end of a sentence and refer back to the sentence.

Here are some of the common smilies and their meanings. Tilt your head to the left to see the faces.

:-)   Smiley face; happiness

;-)   Wink; light sarcasm

:-|	Indifference
:->	Wicked grin; heavy sarcasm
:-D	Shock or surprise
:-/	Perplexity; puzzlement
:-(	Frown; anger or displeasure
:-e	Disappointment

Note that smilies are used only in personal e-mails. They are not considered appropriate for business e-mail.

Source: Suzy Girard, "Was It Something I Typed?" *Success,* February/March 2001, p. 42; "E-Mail Etiquette," http://www.learnthenet.com/english/html/65mailet.htm, accessed February 27, 2003; "E-Mail Etiquette," http://www.iwillfollow.com/emailetiquette.html, accessed February 27, 2003.

Whatever It Takes

Elizabeth Vargas

The one constant in Elizabeth Vargas's childhood was her family. Vargas's father, who was in the Army, moved his family to bases all over the world. Vargas was born in Paterson, New Jersey. By the time she graduated from high school in Stuttgart, Germany, she had lived in Heidelberg, Brussels, Okinawa, Kansas, and San Francisco.

APWIDE WORLD PHOTOS/JENNIFER GRAYLOCK

A life of constant mobility prepared Vargas for the life of a journalist—ready to travel at a moment's notice to the latest story. Vargas studied journalism at the University of Missouri and got her first job there at KOMU-TV. She spent several years as a broadcast journalist at various local TV stations. Vargas recalls that early in her TV career she received mail suggesting that she go back to Mexico. She was very surprised by the letters, not only because of their rudeness but also because her family was originally from Puerto Rico.

In 1993 Vargas made the big move—from local to national broadcasting for NBC News. At the time, she was one of the few Hispanics on national TV news. Her current assignment is with ABC's *20/20* news magazine program. Says Vargas, "There were no Latina or Latino role models." Instead of focusing on being Hispanic, Vargas concentrated on being a good journalist. Her advice to aspiring journalists is to "read, read, read." Interestingly, given her career, Vargas grew up in a home with no TV.

Source: Elinor J. Brecher, "Elizabeth Vargas: Tuning In at the Top," *Hispanic,* June 2002, pp. 24–25; Luis Fernando Llosa, "Elizabeth's Reign," *Latina Magazine,* February 1999; http://www.latina.com/new/magazine/books/99/feb/triunfos.html, accessed March 6, 2003; "Elizabeth Vargas," http://www.abcnews.com, accessed March 6, 2003.

The two communication behaviors can be combined in a diagram, as shown in Figure 5-2. You can see that placing the two behaviors of responsiveness and assertiveness at right angles to each other results in a model with four boxes. When you plot a person's degree of responsiveness and assertiveness, the intersection of the two lines falls in one of the boxes. Each box represents a communication style: thinker, achiever, seller, and relater.

The Thinker

Thinkers are people who tend to be guarded in their interactions with others. Self-control is very important to them. Thinkers don't reveal much of themselves. Rather, they deflect attention from themselves by asking questions of the other person.

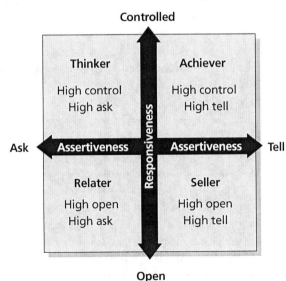

Figure 5-2: A person's communication style can be characterized by the assertiveness and responsiveness he or she shows. By plotting these characteristics on a grid, you can determine the person's communication style.

The Achiever

Like thinkers, achievers are self-controlled and guarded about revealing their inner selves. Achievers are very assertive, however. They express their expectations clearly.

The Seller

Sellers tend to be warm and outgoing in their dealings with others. Like achievers, they are assertive and express themselves forcefully.

The Relater

Relaters are usually warm and friendly in their interactions. They are less concerned about themselves than about others. Relaters ask questions that are sometimes personal in nature.

Understanding the Communication Styles

At one time or another, each of us has used aspects of each communication style. For example, when you communicate with a close friend or spouse, you may be very open and personal (relater). But when you communicate with your boss, you may be very self-controlled and unassertive (thinker). In general, over time, each of us tends to favor one style in most of our interactions with others.

Effective Communication

You can use your knowledge of communication styles to improve the quality of your communication. By identifying your own style and the style of the person with whom you are communicating, you can identify potential communication problems. Once you understand the problems, you can take action to improve your rapport, and consequently your communication, with the other person.

What Is Your Communication Style?

Purpose: You can find out what your dominant communication style is by checking each of the communication characteristics that apply to you. The column with the most check marks represents your preferred communication style.

Thinker

Quiet, level tone of voice _____

Leans back or away _____

Limited eye contact _____

Stiff posture _____

Uses big words _____

Achiever

Factual speech _____

Leans forward and faces others _____

Limited facial expressions _____

Limited body movements _____

Fast-paced speech _____

Relater

Little emphasis on detail _____

Touches others _____

Smiles, nods _____

Casual posture _____

Talks about relationships _____

Seller

Dramatic or loud tone of voice _____

Animated facial expressions _____

Direct eye contact _____

Lots of body and hand movement _____

Uses voice to emphasize points _____

Identifying Communication Problems

You've already identified your own preferred communication style in the previous Your Turn exercise. By listening and observing, you can identify the preferred communication styles of others. By noticing such aspects of their behavior, you can use the communication styles chart to determine other people's preferred communication style.

If a person shows four to five characteristics of a style, he or she has a high preference for it. Two to three characteristics of a style reveal a moderate preference for that style. One characteristic is not significant.

Improving Rapport

How can people with differing communication styles improve the quality of their communication? The answer is they must improve their rapport. In other words, they must become more alike in their communication styles. The way people do this is by imitating one another's behavior, or mirroring.

People do a certain amount of mirroring without being aware of it. If you have ever observed people deep in conversation, you may have noticed that their postures were similar or they both spoke softly. You can take this unconscious process further by paying attention to the other person's behavior and mirroring it. Mirroring does not mean imitation so obvious that the other person notices it. Rather, mirroring consists of subtle, small adjustments in your communication behavior to more closely match your companion. When you mirror successfully, the other person feels that you are in harmony. People are most comfortable with those they feel are like themselves.

Mirroring does not always improve rapport, so there are times it should not be used. For example, mirroring the behavior of someone who is angry or verbally aggressive will only make the interaction escalate. Instead, to calm the tone of the interaction, you can respond in a quiet, evenhanded way.

Map Your Communication

Purpose: Understanding how others communicate can give you tremendous insight about the style in which you interact. This exercise will give you opportunity to compare.

Choose a friend or colleague and observe him or her communicating. Use the indicators in Your Turn 5-2 to decide which style he or she favors and how many indicators he or she shows. Then plot your style and the person's style in the communication effectiveness map below.

1. What is your style?

---

2. What is your friend or colleague's style?

_____

_____

_____

_____

_____

_____

_____

3. Do your styles overlap or touch?

If yes, describe the quality of your communication with this person.

_____

_____

_____

_____

_____

_____

_____

4. Is there a gap between your styles?

If yes, describe any communication problems you may be having.

_____

_____

_____

_____

_____

_____

_____

Mirroring Senses

Each person has a preferred sense, and you can often tell which it is by listening to them talk. Most people prefer the senses of sight, hearing, or touch.

> ➤ Visual people say things like "I'll watch out for that," "It's clear to me," and "I can see that."
> ➤ People who rely on the sense of hearing use phrases such as "That rings a bell," "I hear what you're saying," and "That sounds good to me."
> ➤ People who favor the sense of touch say things like, "This feels right," "I can't get a hold on it," or "I grasp the meaning of that."

A few people rely on the sense of taste or smell.

> ➤ Those who rely on the sense of taste use phrases like "Let me chew on that a while," "That leaves a bad taste in my mouth," or "He's so delectable."
> ➤ People who favor the sense of smell say things like, "That idea stinks," "It seems fishy to me," or "She came out of it smelling like a rose."

When you've determined a person's preferred sense, you can increase your rapport by speaking the same language. For example, if the person is visual, you can ask, "Do you see what I mean?" If the person relies on hearing, you can phrase your question, "Does that sound right to you?"

Overcoming Shyness

Bernardo Carducci, a psychology professor at Indiana University Southwest, has some suggestions to help people overcome shyness with small talk.

> ➤ Before a gathering, think about the people who will be there and what they may discuss.
> ➤ Arrive early. It's easier to start a new conversation than to break into a conversation that's in progress.
> ➤ Start a conversation by talking about something you and the other person share—the place, the weather, the host, and so on. Then introduce yourself.
> ➤ When the other person introduces a topic, support his or her remark. Make a comment on the topic, or throw out another topic.

These small-talk pointers show that you need not be brilliant to be an effective communicator. You simply need to be responsive to other people.

ELEMENTS OF EXCELLENCE

After reading this chapter, you have learned

> ➤ what basic skills are necessary for you to have effective listening and communication skills.
> ➤ how barriers to communication can reduce your ability to connect and relate to others.
> ➤ what your personal communication style is and how to use this knowledge to better interrelate with others.
> ➤ how to map your communications with friends, family, and colleagues.

The Information Highway

Getting Up to Speed

Communication is a huge topic, and finding specific information on the Internet can be difficult unless you narrow your search. Here are Web sites that provide starting-off points:

> ➤ **http://cios.org.** The Communication Institute for Online Scholarship offers resources to students and faculty in the field of communication. To use all its services, you must be a member or attend a school that is a member.
> ➤ **http://members.aol.com.** If you are interested in nonverbal communication, visit the Web site of the Center for Nonverbal Studies. It has links to other interesting sites and maintains a dictionary of nonverbal communication.

You can try searching on your own by using key words such as *nonverbal communication, facial expressions, e-mail etiquette, prejudice,* and *rapport.*

Answer the following journal questions.

1. Describe your family's use of nonverbal communication. What facial expressions, eye contact, and body language are used to communicate in your home?

_____

_____

_____

_____

_____

_____

_____

_____

_____

2. Which of the barriers to communication—physical, mental, or emotional—poses the greatest problem for you? How can you overcome this barrier?

_____

_____

_____

_____

_____

_____

_____

_____

_____

_____

3. Use the communication effectiveness grid and map your communication style and that of your spouse, significant other, or close friend. Are your communication styles similar or different? How does this affect your relationship?

_____

_____

_____

_____

_____

_____

_____

_____

_____

_____

4. If you are shy, make a plan for being more communicative at your next social gathering. If you are not shy, offer advice to a shy friend on how to communicate effectively.

_____

_____

_____

_____

_____

_____

_____

_____

_____

_____

Chapter 6

Improving Your Listening Skills

It is the disease of not listening . . . that I am troubled [with].

WILLIAM SHAKESPEARE,
16TH–17TH CENTURY
ENGLISH DRAMATIST
AND POET

Tanisha was explaining to her friend Joanna why she had decided to quit her job. As Tanisha described the events that led to her decision, Joanna nodded and said, "Uh-huh." When Tanisha finished her story she paused expectantly, waiting for Joanna to say something. Startled by the silence, Joanna said, "Oh, I'm sorry, Tanisha, what were you saying?"

At one time or another, all of us have been in Tanisha's position—exasperated because someone with whom we thought we were communicating was not listening. And we all have been guilty of behaving as Joanna did—seeming to pay attention while our minds were elsewhere. Failing to listen to a friend can damage the friendship. Failing to listen to instructors, bosses, and coworkers has repercussions, too. It can lead to misunderstandings, mistakes, and hard feelings. "If each of America's more than 100 million workers prevented just one $10 mistake by better listening, their organizations would gain over $1 billion in

AP/WIDE WORLD PHOTOS/DELTA DEMOCRAT TIMES, DONALD ADDERTON

Musicians develop excellent listening skills by playing in groups.

< 105 >

profits," says Lyman K. Steil, president of Communication Development Inc., a consulting firm that teaches listening skills.

Because most communication—both personal and professional—involves listening, it's important to improve your listening skills. In this chapter, you will learn why listening is so hard. You will also learn about techniques you can use to become a more effective listener.

Why Is Listening So Hard?

Listening seems like such an easy thing to do. After all, you just have to keep your ears open. But listening is more than hearing. You hear with your ears, but you listen with your brain. Imagine talking with an interesting person at a party. You can hear many conversations in the room, but you are listening to just one.

So why is listening so hard? Listening requires concentration. That means ignoring the hundreds of other things going on around you as well as in your head. Distractions, preconceptions, self-absorption, and daydreaming can all interfere with your ability to listen.

Distractions

It's easy to be distracted when you're listening to someone. Perhaps there's other activity in the room that draws your eyes or ears. Perhaps the person with whom you are speaking is wearing earrings that you can't stop looking at. Or another individual may pace or gesture or exhibit a mannerism that's hard to ignore. Whatever the distraction, it competes with the communication for your attention. And once your attention is divided, it's hard to listen well.

Preconceptions

Preconceptions about the speakers or what they have to say are barriers to effective listening. If you think that the speaker is a fool or has opinions that are the opposite of yours, you may close down your brain and pay no attention. What you lose is an opportunity to learn something—even if your preconceptions turn out to be true. You may even be surprised to hear something of interest if you decide to listen in spite of your presumptions about the speaker or the message.

Self-Absorption

Another cause of poor listening is that you focus on yourself rather than on the person who is talking. Instead of listening carefully to the other person, you are busy thinking about your own agenda. While the individual talks, you are planning and rehearsing your response. In effect, you are just waiting for the other person to be quiet so you can jump in with your contribution to the conversation.

Listening Effectively

> Years ago, I tried to top everybody, but I don't anymore. . . . When you're always trying for a topper, you aren't really listening. It kills communication.
>
> GROUCHO MARX,
> COMEDIAN AND ACTOR

Many people listen with just one ear. They understand just enough of what the speaker is saying to keep the conversation going with nods, smiles, and a well-placed "uh-huh." With these responses, the listener is trying to convince the speaker that he or she is paying attention by being a passive listener.

In most situations, active listening is required when you communicate. Active listening means that your mind is engaged with the message and the speaker. You are concentrating on the speaker, and you are participating in the communication.

There are many techniques you can use to practice active listening. These techniques include being physically prepared, being open to the other person, being curious, asking questions, and listening for the meaning of the words and the unspoken message.

> He heard it, but he heeded not—his eyes were with his heart, and that was far away.
>
> LORD BYRON,
> 19TH-CENTURY
> ENGLISH POET

Be Open

The Japanese symbol for the word *listen* shows the character for "ear" placed within the character for "gate." When we listen to someone, we are in effect passing through the other person's gate and entering his or her world. When we listen effectively, we are receiving the speaker's message in an open, nonjudgmental way.

Being willing to accept the speaker's message means that you stop focusing on finding contradictions and errors. Instead, you let the message get through. Then you can evaluate the message—after you've actually listened to it.

If you can listen openly, you will communicate to the speaker that you think he or she is important and has ideas worth hearing. You communicate an attitude of respect for the other person. The bonus of open listening is that the speaker will feel less defensive and more open to you.

Be Curious

> It is the province of knowledge to speak and the privilege of wisdom to listen.
>
> OLIVER WENDELL HOLMES, 19TH-CENTURY AUTHOR AND PHYSICIAN

Part of being an open listener is being curious about other people. If you can really listen to what another person has to say, you will find that you can learn a lot. Try to be observant and objective about listening, and you will be able to gather a great deal of information. To do this, you must let your curiosity overcome your need to judge the other person and justify your own position.

Ask Questions

You can express your curiosity about the speaker as well as clarify your understanding of the message by asking questions. Effective listeners ask questions in a way that will elicit informative answers.

How Good a Listener Are You?

Purpose: This exercise will help you to determine how effective of a listener you are.

Take a moment to think about your own qualities as a listener. Then answer the following questions to see what your strengths and weaknesses are.

	Yes	No
1. Is your hearing normal?	☐	☐
2. Do you look at the person who is speaking?	☐	☐
3. Do you try to ignore other sights and sounds when you listen to someone speak?	☐	☐

	Yes	No
4. While listening, do you avoid doing something else at the same time (like reading or watching TV)?	☐	☐
5. When someone is talking to you, do you concentrate on him or her rather than on your own thoughts?	☐	☐
6. Do you think that other people can teach you something?	☐	☐
7. If you don't understand something, do you ask the speaker to repeat it?	☐	☐
8. Do you listen even when you disagree with what the speaker is saying?	☐	☐
9. If you think the subject is dull or too hard, do you tune out?	☐	☐
10. Do you frequently have to ask people to repeat themselves because you've forgotten what they have said?	☐	☐
11. If the speaker's appearance or manner is poor, do you pay less attention?	☐	☐
12. Do you pretend to pay attention even when you are not listening?	☐	☐

If you answered yes to the first eight questions and no to the last four questions, your listening skills are good. Even if you got a perfect score, the tips and techniques that follow will help you improve your listening skills.

In general, the most effective questions are open-ended questions. Open-ended questions cannot be answered with just a yes or a no; they require an explanation as a response. Questions that begin with what, how, and why are

> If you wish to know the mind of a man, listen to his words.
>
> CHINESE PROVERB

generally open-ended questions. For example, "What happened at the meeting?" "How do you feel about that?" and "Why did he leave?" are questions that require an informative response. Open-ended questions are used to get more detail and to clarify messages.

On the other hand, closed-ended questions can be answered with a simple yes or no. "Did you agree with her?" and "Do you like it?" are examples of closed-ended questions. Closed-ended questions tend to limit the exchange of information, especially when the speaker is shy or reserved. Effective listeners can use closed-ended questions, however, when information needs to be checked. "Do you mean you'll be a day late?" is a closed-ended question that verifies the listener's understanding of the message.

> We have two ears and one mouth that we may listen the more and talk the less.
>
> ZENO, ANCIENT GREEK PHILOSOPHER

Remember, good questions, both open- and closed-ended, arise out of the conversation. That means that you, the listener, must be paying attention. The next time you watch someone doing an interview on television, notice whether they stick to a script of questions, no matter what the response, or whether they allow their questions to arise from the content of the interview. Good interviewers are good listeners, and their questions are relevant to the conversation.

Listen for Meaning and Verbal Cues

We mentioned earlier that listeners can understand verbal messages far faster than speakers can say them. Rather than using the brain's down time for daydreaming, effective listeners use it to think about the meaning of what they hear.

Try to identify the ideas and facts and the relationships between them. Ask yourself, What is the most important thing being said? What facts or ideas support the main idea? Does one thing cause another? Is sequence or time involved? Does this represent a fact or an opinion? Thinking critically about the message will help you understand it and keep your attention focused on the communication.

In addition, thinking about the meaning of the speaker's message can give you cues about your own responses. For example, if you are being interviewed for a job, you should listen carefully to what the interviewer is saying. If the interviewer talks a lot about the company's reputation for high-quality service, you can describe your own commitment to high quality in some aspect of your life. If the interviewer asks an open-ended question, give a full response.

Listening: A Cornerstone of Psychotherapy

A woman in her late thirties was having marital and family problems, and she went to a psychotherapist for help. Here is a brief excerpt from one of their sessions.

Woman: You know this is kind of goofy, but I've never told anyone this and it'll probably do me good. . . . For years . . . I have had . . . "flashes of sanity" . . . wherein I really feel sane . . . .and pretty much aware of life. . . .

Therapist: It's been fleeting and it's been infrequent, but there have been times when it seems the whole you is functioning and feeling in the world, a very chaotic world to be sure. . . .

Woman: That's right. . . .

Notice how the therapist took the woman's first statement and rephrased it, trying to clarify her meaning. He must have been listening carefully. All psychotherapy involves close listening, but in client-centered psychotherapy listening is a crucial tool.

In client-centered psychotherapy, the therapists try to help clients release their ability to understand and manage their lives—what we have been calling reaching your potential. According to psychologist Carl Rogers, this personal growth will occur if three conditions exist in the relationship between therapist and client:

1. The therapist must be thoroughly herself or himself by expressing feelings and attitudes toward the client, not opinions or judgments. By being open with the client, the therapist builds the client's trust.
2. The therapist must accept the client as he or she is—a condition known as unconditional positive regard. By doing so, the therapist shows care for the client, no matter what the client is feeling or thinking.
3. The therapist must aim for a thorough, empathic understanding of the client through active listening. By clarifying the meaning of what the client is saying, the therapist can promote the client's even deeper understanding of self.

This last component of client-centered therapy is based on listening. "Therapists can learn, quite quickly, to be better, more sensitive listeners, more empathic. It is in part a skill as well as an attitude," says Rogers.

How can client-centered therapy help people? According to Rogers, when clients find a therapist listening to and accepting their thoughts and feelings, they are better able to accept their own thoughts and feelings—even the negative ones. This increased acceptance leads to a feeling of having greater self-control. As clients become more self-aware and self-accepting, they find some of the freedom to grow and change as a human being.

Source: Carl Rogers, *On Personal Power: Inner Strength and Its Revolutionary Impact,* New York: Delacorte, 1977, pp. 9–12; *On Becoming a Person,* Boston: Houghton Mifflin, 1961, pp. 61–62, 89.

PITFALLS

The Impact of Technology and "Listening"

More and more it is becoming common for business to be transacted in countless mediums beyond face-to-face communication. Phone conversations and e-mail are areas in which it becomes easier and more tempting to listen less closely. Many people carry on phone conversations while engaging in one or more other actions, reducing their ability to listen effectively. E-mail is increasingly replacing face-to-face conversation, and is an ineffective form of communicating two-sided information. Be aware of how you interact in both of these mediums.

Listen between the Lines

Effective listening requires more than just paying attention to the words. An active listener also focuses on nonverbal cues. By paying attention to the nonverbal aspects of communication, you can improve your ability to listen.

Most nonverbal communication cues are visual, so it's important for the listener to be able to see the speaker. You can get a sense of how sight contributes to effective listening by comparing the experiences of talking face to face and over the telephone. When you talk face to face, you can perceive the person's feelings and unstated messages by looking at the other person's face, eyes, and gestures. In contrast, when you listen on the telephone, you rely on your ears to pick up both the words and the voice cues. Your ability to detect the unstated message is reduced because you cannot see the speaker. When you communicate by e-mail or instant messaging, you lose both sight and voice cues and depend entirely on words for meaning.

> Everything becomes possible by the mere presence of someone who knows how to listen, to love, and to give of himself.
>
> ELIE WIESEL, HOLOCAUST SURVIVOR AND WRITER

Take Notes

Another way to ensure that you listen actively is to take notes. Taking notes forces you to pay attention to the message and decide what's important enough to write down. As we discussed in Chapter 3, taking and reviewing notes also helps you remember what you hear.

Although you may be used to taking notes in class, there are other situations in which note taking is a good way to ensure effective listening. When you are listening to directions, for example, it's helpful to write them down. When you are doing business on the phone, take notes about the details. That way you'll be sure to get the message accurately and completely.

Whatever It Takes

Chan Ho Yun

When Kika Keith looked for music lessons for her daughter, she found that Colburn, a famous performing arts school in downtown Los Angeles, was too far away from her neighborhood. Private violin lessons there were too expensive as well. But she also found Chan Ho Yun at Colburn. A violinist and teacher, Yun offered Keith a deal. If Keith would find space in her neighborhood and more kids to take lessons, he would teach them free of charge.

So began Sweet Strings, a classical music program for the kids of South Central Los Angeles. For Keith, the way Sweet Strings took off was a

COURTESY OF TANNERY HILL STUDIOS

complete surprise. South Central, better known for its rap fans, turned out to have a lot of classical music lovers, too. When word of free violin lessons got around the neighborhood, people flocked to join the program. The first class, in 1999, had 25 children and no instruments. By 2000, there were 60 students and 50 donated violins. Soon the program was giving free violin, viola, cello, and bass lessons to over 100 African American, Latino, and Korean kids, with a waiting list of more than 300.

Today Sweet Strings relies on donations from Hollywood celebrities, large corporations, and foundations. It has some paid as well as volunteer music teachers. Because their resources are limited, Sweet Strings can't admit everyone. They accept the students with the greatest need—those whose schools do not have a music program. Students from Sweet Strings have played at the opening night of the Hollywood Bowl and at an event at which President Clinton was the featured speaker.

As the children learn music, the community has also benefited in other ways. Yun required that parents accompany their children to lessons. So parents learned to read music, too. In addition, they got to know their neighbors. People of different backgrounds found that stereotypes were breaking down and friendships were forming because of the shared interest in children and music. Says Yun, "No matter where we come from or what color we are, the only color I recognize is the color of the sound of the music we make."

Source: Amy Reeves, "Sweet Strings in South Central L.A.," *Strings,* January 2001, no. 91, http://www.stringsmagazine.com/issues/strings91/Newsprof.shtml, accessed February 28, 2003; Christina Cheakalos and Caren Grigsby Bates, "Strings of His Heart," *People,* March 19, 2001, pp. 69–70; "Chan Ho Yun, Violin Teacher and Performer, Cofounder, Sweet Strings," http://www.digitalheroes.org/dhc/bios/bio_yun.html, accessed February 28, 2003.

•

 ## ELEMENTS OF EXCELLENCE

After reading this chapter, you have learned

> ➤ why listening is so difficult and how to eliminate key challenges.
> ➤ where your personal strengths and challenges lie in regards to your listening skills.
> ➤ about key strategies that will help you to increase your ability to listen.

Getting Up to Speed

There is a wealth of information about listening skills on the Internet, ranging from sales pitches for listening seminars to sites posting suggestions for improving listening skills.

> **http://listen.org.** A good place to start is the International Listening Association's site, which has links to listening resources.

> **http://www.hearnet.com.** For resources on hearing protection and hearing aids, check the Web site of HEAR (Hearing Education and Awareness for Rockers), a nonprofit organization started by a rock musician who suffered hearing loss.

> **http://www.eslcafe.com.** Dave's ESL Café on the Web is a comprehensive site of interest to speakers of English as a second language. Their search engine provides links to ESL listening resources on the Internet.

In addition, to learn more about topics in this chapter, you can do searches using the key words *listening skills, hearing education, client-centered psychotherapy, Carl Rogers,* and *noise.*

JOURNAL

Answer the following journal questions.

1. What barriers to listening interfere with your ability to listen effectively? How can you overcome these barriers?

_____

_____

_____

_____

_____

_____

_____

_____

2. In what situations do you find yourself not paying attention to a speaker? How can you be more open to hearing the messages of others?

_____

_____

_____

_____

_____

_____

3. What role does listening play in your life at home? At work? In which situation is your listening most effective? Why?

_____

_____

_____

_____

_____

_____

4. If you improved your listening skill at school, how would this benefit you?

_____

_____

_____

_____

_____

_____

Chapter 7

Improving Your Speaking Skills

A loud voice cannot compete with a clear voice, even if it's a whisper.

BARRY NEIL KAUFMAN

From the time you get up in the morning until you go to sleep at night, you use your voice to communicate. At home you converse with your family about the events of the day. With your friends you talk about whatever concerns you. You use the telephone to speak about business and personal matters. At school you ask and answer questions in class and talk with other students. At work you give directions, explain things, ask and answer questions, participate in meetings, and talk with customers and coworkers. You may occasionally give oral presentations at school or work.

Because talking is the basic form of communication among people, you are judged to a great extent by your ability to speak. People recognize you by your speech. The words you choose, your gestures, the expressions on your face, the sound of your voice, and the way you pronounce words add up to an instantly recognizable person. The way you speak is an expression of your personality. In this chapter, you will learn that speaking

COURTESY OF CLIFF HOLLIS, EAST CAROLINA UNIVERSITY

People with speech problems understand the value of speaking skills. Joseph Kalinowski, a speech pathology professor, has been stuttering since childhood. He helped develop a small device, worn in the ear, that suppresses stuttering.

involves more than words. You will discover that your appearance, your voice qualities, and how you say things all have a great impact on the people around you. You will learn techniques for effective face-to-face and telephone conversations. Last, you will learn some ways to improve your ability to speak to groups, both informally and formally.

First Impressions

Speaking is not limited to the words you say. In addition to the words of your message, listeners perceive the way you look and the way you sound. In studies of face-to-face communication, Dr. Albert Mehrabian has found that the impact on the listener of appearance and voice is far greater than that of words (see Figure 7-1). In fact, since listeners see you before they hear you, your appearance has a great effect on your ability to get your message across. You have seven to ten seconds to make a good first impression!

If people's visual impression of you is poor, they are less likely to listen to what you have to say. Most people are put off by bad posture, lack of cleanliness, and sloppiness. Good posture, hygiene, and grooming are essential to forming a favorable first impression.

Also important in creating a good first impression is the way you dress. In recent years, dress standards have changed considerably. It's no longer possible to prescribe appropriate dress for every situation. Rather, you should think of your listeners. If their opinions are important to you, then you should dress in a way that is acceptable to them. Whatever type of clothing you decide on, it should be clean and neat. Your clothes should not distract your listeners from your message.

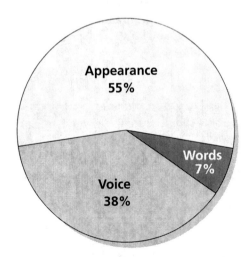

Figure 7-1: Your appearance and voice have far more impact on your listeners than what you actually say.

Speech Qualities

Once your listeners have gotten a first impression of you from your appearance, they get their second impression from your speech. Most people want to be perceived as intelligent, competent, and attractive. To be perceived this way, you must speak well. You must control the qualities of your voice—volume, pitch, rate, and tone. You must pronounce words accurately; enunciate, or speak clearly; and use correct grammar and appropriate vocabulary.

In the United States, there are four basic varieties of spoken American English: standard English, dialects, accented English, and substandard English.

1. Standard English is the English spoken by national news broadcasters, actors, and others who have rid themselves of regional or social dialects.
2. Dialects are variations of American English that are spoken in particular areas or by particular social groups. The most familiar regional dialects are those of the South, New York City, Boston, and the Midwest. Black English, a dialect spoken by many African Americans, is found in all regions of the United States. It is sometimes called Ebonics.
3. Accented English is spoken by the many Americans for whom English is a second language.
4. Substandard English is English spoken with poor pronunciation, enunciation, grammar, and vocabulary.

TIPS

Getting to Know Standard English

Largely through the influence of television, standard English is easily understood throughout the United States. It has therefore become the norm against which people's speech is judged. Since the purpose of speaking is to communicate, it makes sense to communicate in language that people from all social groups and regions of the country understand. So if you are trying to improve your speech, you should be imitating the standard English you hear on national news broadcasts. As you practice improving various aspects of your speech, you should try to record your voice so you can hear what you sound like.

Volume

The volume of your voice refers to its intensity or loudness. In most situations, a moderate volume is appropriate for standard English and will enable listeners to hear you. Of course, if you are addressing a large group, you will have to raise the volume of your voice or use a microphone. In addition, a good speaker uses changes in volume to emphasize parts of the message.

If you are having trouble speaking loudly enough, you should practice breathing properly. If you take quick, shallow breaths, your lungs do not have enough air to produce sounds loud enough to be heard easily. Instead, you should breathe deeply and control your breath as singers and actors do.

Pitch

Pitch refers to the level of sound on a musical scale. People who speak with a high-pitched voice sound shrill and unpleasant. On the other hand, people whose voices are pitched too low can be hard to hear. And people whose pitch never varies speak in a monotone, which is boring for listeners. A moderate pitch with variations is best for standard English.

Pitch carries different meanings in standard English and regional dialects. For example, when you ask a question in standard English, the pitch of your voice rises toward the end of the sentence. The rising pitch at the end of the sentence conveys a question, doubt, or hesitation. Since a rising pitch at the end of a sentence means uncertainty in standard English, many Northerners are confused when they listen to people speaking a Southern dialect. Southerners have a slight rise in pitch at the ends of most sentences. This rise doesn't mean uncertainty; rather it's meant to convey courtesy, a meaning that's lost on Northerners. You can see from this small example that using standard English can prevent the miscommunication that results when dialect differences are not understood.

> Words mean more than what is set down on paper. It takes the human voice to infuse them with shades of deeper meaning.
>
> MAYA ANGELOU,
> AFRICAN AMERICAN
> AUTHOR

Rate

Standard English is spoken at a moderate rate. Indeed, because of the long vowel sounds in English, it's hard to speak the language very quickly. As with pitch, there are regional differences in the rate of speech. Northerners tend to speak faster than Southerners, and people from the Northeast speak faster than those from the Midwest.

To avoid sounding boring, you can vary the rate of your speech. You can slow down to emphasize important facts or ideas or to accommodate a listener who can't keep up with you. You can also pause to emphasize major points. A moment of silence has the power to refocus your listener's attention. Avoid filling your pauses with sounds like "um" and "uh." These fillers are distracting to your listeners.

Tone

As you know, tone of voice reveals the speaker's feelings and attitudes. A voice can be depressed, cheerful, angry, or neutral. Because tone of voice is so revealing, you should be aware of what you sound like. Sometimes it's appropriate to convey your emotions through the tone of your voice. For example, you may want to communicate your happiness that your friend is getting married. At other times you may want to change your tone to avoid communicating a feeling you would rather hide. You may wish to sound neutral rather than angry, for instance, when you are disagreeing with your boss.

Enunciation

Enunciation refers to the clarity with which you say words. Saying "didja" for "did you" or "talkin'" for "talking" are examples of poor enunciation. Poor enunciation is the result of leaving out sounds, adding sounds, and running sounds together. Poor enunciation in standard English may be the result of speaking a regional dialect.

Commonly left out sounds are the final *t, g,* and *d* when they follow another consonant. For example, many people say "stric" rather than "strict," "goin'" rather than "going," and "pon" rather than "pond." Some vowels are frequently swallowed as well. When two vowel sounds occur together, one is often lost. For example, many people say "pome" rather than "poem" and "crule" rather than "cruel." Sometimes entire syllables are lost, as in "praps" for "perhaps" and "lil" for "little."

Another type of poor enunciation is the addition of unnecessary sounds. "Umberella" for "umbrella," "disasterous" for "disastrous," and "exshtra" for "extra" are some examples. Finally, slurring words—saying them indistinctly and running them together—makes you difficult to understand. "C'mere, I wancha t'gimmee a hand" is an example of slurred speech. Unless you enunciate clearly, your listeners may pay more attention to decoding your speech than to interpreting its meaning.

Pronunciation

Pronunciation is closely related to enunciation. Whereas enunciation refers to the clarity with which you say words, pronunciation refers to the correctness with which you say words. A person who says "Febyuary" instead of "February" or stresses the wrong syllable in "harassment" is mispronouncing words. Many pronunciation errors in English arise from the quirks of spelling. The *t* in "often," for example, is not pronounced. The letters *ea* sound different in "break" and "beak." In addition, some words have more than one acceptable pronunciation.

Grammar and Vocabulary

You may enunciate clearly and pronounce words correctly, but if you've chosen the wrong words or put them together incorrectly, you will not be considered a good communicator. A good vocabulary allows you to present your thoughts with precision.

Justly or not, people who constantly make grammatical errors when speaking standard English are considered poorly educated and unprofessional. If you think your grammar could use improvement, try reading more. By reading you will absorb many of the rules of standard English grammar. If you think you need more help than that, you can enroll in a course at your school or an adult education center.

YOUR TURN 7-1

Rate Your Speech Qualities

Purpose: There are many different elements to consider when evaluating your ability to speak. This exercise will help you to understand what areas you are strong in when it comes to speech, and which areas need development.

Answer the following questions to evaluate your speech qualities. You may have to ask a friend to help you if you're not sure how you sound.

	Yes	No
1. I usually speak standard English.	☐	☐
2. I speak at a moderate volume, neither too loud nor too soft.	☐	☐

	Yes	No
3. I speak at a moderate pitch and vary the pitch to convey different meanings.	☐	☐
4. I speak at a moderate rate, neither too fast nor too slow.	☐	☐
5. I use pauses to emphasize major points.	☐	☐
6. I control the tone of my voice in order to better communicate my messages.	☐	☐
7. I usually enunciate clearly and distinctly.	☐	☐
8. When I'm not sure of the pronunciation of a word, I look it up in a dictionary.	☐	☐
9. I use a wide range of words when speaking.	☐	☐
10. When I speak, I use correct grammar.	☐	☐

A no answer to any of these questions indicates that you can improve your speech. ▩

Effective Conversations

An attractive appearance and good speech contribute to your effectiveness as a communicator, but they are not enough to ensure good communication. In face-to-face communication, it's important to think as much of the

> A rumor goes in one ear and out many mouths.
> CHINESE PROVERB

person with whom you are conversing as you do about yourself and your message. So in addition to knowing what you want to communicate, you must make others feel comfortable by establishing a positive atmosphere, using appropriate body language, listening, letting others speak, and mirroring their speech.

Know What You Want to Say

If a conversation has a purpose other than social chitchat, you should be mentally prepared for it. That means you know beforehand what message you want to communicate. You have decided what points you need to cover and what your approach will be. When you are mentally prepared, instead of floundering, you will be able to direct the conversation where you want it to go. There's another side to knowing what you want to say, and that's knowing what you don't want to say. It's important to respect confidences and to be discreet and tactful. Communicating private matters to people who are not directly concerned will eventually result in your being perceived as untrustworthy and rude. To avoid this, make sure you keep confidences and speak to others with tact and discretion.

> One of the greatest pleasures of life is conversation.
>
> SYDNEY SMITH, 19TH-CENTURY ENGLISH CLERGYMAN AND WRITER

Establish a Positive Atmosphere

The environment of a conversation has a great effect on the quality of the communication that takes place. No one would expect to have a mutually satisfying conversation, for example, in a police interrogation room with bright lights trained on the suspect. Sitting behind a large desk or in an imposing chair or standing over the person with whom you're conversing sends a similar message: You are in control. Any setup that makes the speaker appear dominant has the effect of stifling the free flow of communication.

So if you want to converse openly and honestly with someone, be sure that the environment contributes to a relaxed atmosphere. Make sure there are no physical barriers between you and your listener. Move out from behind a table or desk, sit if the listener is sitting, and move the furniture to get comfortable seating if necessary.

Use Body Language

You are already aware of how much facial expressions, eye contact, posture, and gestures can communicate. When you speak, try to use the vocabulary of body language to add to the meaning of your verbal message. Smiling, looking people in the eye, holding yourself tall but relaxed, and gesturing for emphasis will help hold the attention of your listeners. On the other hand, do not exaggerate your use of body language, because that is distracting. It's also important to control any mannerisms you may have, such as biting the end of a pen or playing with objects in your hands.

Listen

Nothing conveys your interest in the other person as much as listening carefully to what he or she has to say. Your success as a speaker is dependent on your effectiveness as a listener. Only if you listen carefully will you get feedback to your message. And good feedback is necessary to keep a conversation effective.

> Silent? Ah, he is silent! He can keep silence well. That man's silence is wonderful to listen to.
>
> THOMAS HARDY,
> 19TH-CENTURY
> ENGLISH NOVELIST

Let Others Talk

A conversation is a dialogue, not a monologue. If you monopolize the conversation, you will find that effective communication is not taking place. Part of being a good speaker is knowing when to let the other person talk. Be attentive to your listener so you will know when he or she wants to say something. Then be silent and listen.

Mirror the Speech of Others

As you recall, people are most comfortable communicating with those who are like themselves. Part of establishing rapport with another person is to mirror aspects of their communication style. When you have a conversation, you can mirror the speech of the other person. You can match the pace, pitch, tone, or volume of others' speech, the words they use, and their body language. Mirroring aspects of the other person's communication style will help the person relax and be more open with you.

In addition to reacting to the other person's communication style, you can affect that style by your actions. For example, suppose you are talking to someone who speaks very slowly. You can try to speed him up by mirroring his pace, then gradually speaking faster. Without even being aware of it, he will speed up a bit to match you. If you want someone to relax, make sure your own posture is relaxed, your voice is calm, and your facial expression interested and pleasant.

Speaking on the Telephone

The visual dimension of communication is lost when you talk on the telephone. The power of facial expressions, eye contact, and gestures to communicate is gone. Instead, you must rely on your words and voice to convey your message. You must concentrate on identifying yourself and being courteous and attentive in order to communicate effectively on the telephone. Do not assume you know what is being perceived by your listener. Clarify what you are intending to communicate consistently.

> It takes two to speak the truth— one to speak, and another to hear.
>
> HENRY DAVID THOREAU, 19TH-CENTURY AUTHOR AND NATURALIST

Telephone Tips

Telephones, answering machines, and voice mail are everywhere, and you have been using them for years. But do you use this technology properly? Here are some tips to help you master the telephone.

> Speak directly into the mouthpiece of the telephone, with your lips about an inch from the phone. Don't let the telephone slip below your chin. The listener will have trouble hearing you, or your voice may not be properly recorded on an answering machine or voice mail system.

> If you are using a speaker phone, face the unit so your voice will be picked up properly.

> Speak at a normal volume. It's usually not necessary to shout. If the connection is bad, place the call again.

> Enunciate clearly so you will be understood.

> If you get a wrong number, don't just hang up. Apologize for the mistake. Not only is this good manners but also it protects your reputation for professionalism. Remember that many phones have caller ID and you can be identified.

> If you have to leave the line, tell the other person what you are doing. Inform her if you are putting her on hold or responding to a call-waiting signal. If you are gone more than a minute, check back and ask if

she would like to continue to hold. That tells her that she hasn't been forgotten.

> Don't drop the receiver or put it down hard on a table or desk. The noise it makes is amplified and will disturb the person at the other end of the line.

> When you hang up, gently put the receiver in its cradle.

Wanted: Bilingual Workers

"What is an extra language worth?" That question is being asked all over the country by bilingual workers. As American companies and governments do more business with non-English speakers, the demand for bilingual employees is rising. Bilingual workers are needed in health care, technology, social work, teaching, public safety, and administrative jobs in both the private and public sector.

Being bilingual in today's job market is a plus. Many employers want to hire employees who are bilingual and bicultural as well, meaning that they understand the language, customs, and traditions of foreign-born customers. A survey conducted by Hispanic Times Enterprises revealed that, when two people with equal qualifications apply for a job and one of them is bilingual, most companies will hire the bilingual applicant. In some places, the need for extra languages is so great that local governments are beginning to mandate the hiring of bilingual workers. For example, in 2001, the city of Oakland, California, passed an ordinance requiring that bilingual workers be hired. Oakland was looking for people who were bilingual in Spanish or Chinese for positions, including police officer, firefighter, sanitation worker, and recreation worker, that involve contact with the public.

But will the bilingual employee be paid more for his or her language skills? Some bilingual employees are paid more, especially those with higher-level jobs. Bilingual financial analysts, merchant bankers, stockbrokers, and middle- and upper-level managers are often paid extra for their relevant language skills. For lower-level jobs, the situation varies considerably, although the trend is toward extra pay. For example, MCI pays its bilingual telephone operators a 10 percent bonus if they speak another language more than half the time on the job. Clark County, Nevada, is planning to pay its bilingual workers an extra $100 a month if at least 20 percent of their work involves dealing with Spanish-speaking clients.

Whether bilingual workers are paid more sometimes depends on whether a second language is considered a job requirement or just an added talent. For example, at MCI knowledge of a second language is a job requirement for certain operator positions, and so these positions pay more.

Whether bilingual employees are paid more also depends on the regional job market. In Miami, Florida, so many people speak both English and Spanish that companies don't need to pay extra to attract bilingual employees. On the other hand, in San Francisco, a Charles Schwab & Company broker who speaks Chinese is paid a higher base salary than other brokers, because this language skill is relatively rare among brokers.

If you are bilingual and want to use your language skills, the Internet will make your job search easier. In addition to checking general-purpose jobs sites, you can check a national database of bilingual job opportunities at http://www.bilingual-jobs.com. You can search there for jobs by language, by location (including international jobs), by company, and by key word.

Source: Rich Heinz, "Employers Eager to Buy Lingual Skills," *California Job Journal,* September 2, 2001, http://www.jobjournal.com/article_printer.asp?artid=333, accessed March 4, 2003; Timothy Pratt, "Plan to Increase Pay for Bilingual Workers Closer to Fruition," *Las Vegas Sun,* July 26, 2002, http://www.lasvegassun.com/sunbin/stories/text/2002/jul/26/513768608.html, accessed March 4, 2003; Peter Fritsch, "Bilingual Employees Are Seeking More Pay, and Many Now Get It," *Wall Street Journal,* November 13, 1996, pp. A1, A15; Elaine McShulskis, "Bilingual Employees More Valuable," *Human Resources Magazine,* April 1996, p. 16; Jane M. Rifkin, "The Competitive Edge," *Hispanic Times Magazine,* December/January 1996, p. 10.

Using Automated Telephone Systems

When you make a call these days, you are as likely to get a machine as a person on the other end of the line. So it pays to be prepared. If you are making a personal call and an answering machine or voice mail system picks up, you can just leave your name, number, and a brief message. However, if you are making a business or information call, be ready to deal with an automated telephone system. Here are some suggestions to help you get the most from these computerized systems.

> To speak, and to speak well, are two things.
>
> BEN JONSON,
> 17TH-CENTURY ENGLISH
> DRAMATIST AND POET

> ➤ Have a pencil and paper handy. You may be given some menu choices depending on the purpose of your call;

for example, "For account balances, press 2." Jot down the choices so you can pick the best one.

> Have all the information you will need right by the telephone. If you have to enter information such as an account or personal identification number, have it handy. It's hard to ask a computer to hold on while you go look for something.

If you wind up going around and around an automated system without accomplishing anything, don't give up. Just hold on or try pressing 0. Eventually a human being may answer!

> The telephone gives us the happiness of being together yet safely apart.
>
> MASON COOLEY,
> AMERICAN APHORIST

Using a Cell Phone

As more people use cell phones, a whole new set of etiquette issues has arisen. Nearly everyone has had the experience of being interrupted by a cell phone ringing at a movie or religious service or on a bus or train. Beyond the distraction of the phone ringing is the distraction of having to listen to someone's cell phone conversation.

Because cell phones are relatively new, people are still working out the social rules that apply to their use. The level of public irritation at cell phone use is so great that policies and legislation are being considered to ban their use in classrooms, theaters, restaurants, and public transportation. Some places have already made it illegal to talk on a cell phone and drive, which is a matter of safety rather than etiquette.

Regardless of the law, it makes sense to use a cell phone without disturbing others. Here are some suggestions.

> Never take or make a personal call during a business meeting, including interviews. If you are expecting an emergency call, set the ringer to vibrate and excuse yourself to answer the phone.
> Don't use a cell phone in lecture halls, elevators, libraries, museums, restaurants, theaters, waiting rooms, places of worship, buses, trains, or other indoor public spaces.
> Don't talk on the phone while conducting personal business, such as banking.
> Keep conversations brief.
> Use an earpiece in noisy places so you can hear how loud you sound and modulate your voice.

> Tell callers you are on a cell phone so they are not surprised by being disconnected.
> Don't set your ringer to a loud or annoying tune.

Talking to a Person on the Telephone

Identify Yourself

Because you cannot be seen, the first step of any telephone conversation is to greet the other person and identify yourself. Even if the person you are calling has caller ID, he or she may not recognize your phone number when it is displayed. So, identification is still needed. If you do not do this immediately, the conversation may be confusing to your listener, who is trying to figure out who you are.

> He has occasional flashes of silence that make his conversation perfectly delightful.
>
> SYDNEY SMITH,
> 19TH-CENTURY ENGLISH
> CLERGYMAN AND WRITER

Be Courteous and Attentive

Courtesy and attention are the basics of effective telephone conversations. Courtesy conveys your interest in, and respect for, the person with whom you are speaking. And attentiveness is needed to listen effectively and communicate well.

Courtesy can be communicated by the words you speak as well as by your tone of voice. If you are calling to conduct business, be sure you make any requests in a polite way. Keep your voice pleasant and friendly so the listener knows you want to be helpful.

Attentiveness is especially important when you speak on the telephone. It's easy to be distracted by what's going on around you or to work on other tasks, since the other person can't see that your attention has wandered. To communicate your attentiveness, you can't rely on body language as you would in face-to-face communication. Rather, you must use your voice to indicate you are paying attention. Instead of nodding, for example, you can say, "I see" or "yes." If the content of the call is important, take notes. Your notes will help you be sure you have a complete and accurate understanding of what's been communicated.

Gary Locke

Growing up in the housing projects of Seattle, Washington, Gary Locke didn't learn to speak English until he started kindergarten. At home with his parents, brothers, and sisters, he spoke Chinese. Today, Gary Locke is the first Chinese American governor of a U.S. state. "The family is very proud," he said. "It really is the American dream."

Over a hundred years ago, Locke's grand-father came to the United States and worked as a house boy in Olympia, Washington, before returning to China. Locke's father emigrated to the United States, fought in the U.S. Army during World War II, and settled in Seattle. Gary was the second of five children the Lockes raised in a housing project for veterans. Locke's parents ran a small grocery store that was open 365 days a year. To keep busy, Locke joined the Boy Scouts and became an Eagle Scout at the age of 14. Locke attributes his rise to governor of Washington to education. "Education is the great equalizer," he said on the night he was elected. Locke paid for college through financial aid, scholarships, and part-time jobs. After college, Locke went to law school and then returned to Washington.

His family hoped he would pursue a career in law or medicine, but Locke entered politics. His family was disappointed but became his biggest supporters when he ran for office as a Washington state legislator. He served 11 years in the state legislature and 3 years as county executive of King County before being elected governor in 1996 and again in 2000. Locke lived in the governor's mansion in Olympia, the capital of Washington, less than a mile from the house where his grandfather worked as a house boy.

Sources: "Our Governor," State of Washington Web site, http://www.governor.wa.gov/, accessed March 6, 2003; Bill Donahue, Don Campbell, and Tina Kelley, "American Tale: Washington Governor Gary Locke Explores His Roots in Jilong, China," *People*, November 24, 1997, pp. 169–170; Timothy Egan, "The 1996 Elections: The States—The Governors; Chinese Roots of Winner Delight the Pacific Rim," *New York Times*, November 7, 1996, p. B8; Rachel Zimmerman, "Chinese Village Swells with Pride as Washington Governor Seeks His Roots on a Pilgrimage," *New York Times*, October 12, 1997, p. A14.

Speaking to Groups

Many people are perfectly comfortable speaking over the phone to one person but find speaking to groups very difficult. Yet since so many of our activities are accomplished in groups—social, educational, and business—it's important to learn to speak well in group situations. Most of the time you will find yourself speaking informally as you participate in a group activity. Occasionally, you may be asked to make a formal presentation to a group.

Speaking Informally in a Group

Whether it's a professional orginization, committee, or meeting of coworkers, the chances are that at least once a day you will find yourself communicating in a group. People who are good at speaking in groups have a great deal of influence over the actions of the group. Good speakers are generally well prepared, assertive, and courteous.

Be Prepared

Preparation is the first prerequisite of effective participation in groups. You cannot speak well unless you know something about the topic under discussion. To prepare for group discussions, you must keep abreast of the subjects that are likely to come up by paying attention to the news and reading trade or professional publications.

Before some meetings, the person leading the meeting distributes an agenda. If you have an agenda, study it before the meeting and learn more about things with which you are unfamiliar. If you don't have an agenda, try to find out before the meeting what subjects are to be covered.

Be Assertive

You may be thoroughly prepared, but unless you speak up you will not contribute to a group's efforts. Speaking up in a group requires assertiveness, the self-belief and determination to make your opinions heard. To be assertive, you must believe that you have something worth saying. You must have confidence in your own ability to contribute to the group.

Being assertive also means you must achieve a balance between your own right to be heard and the rights of others to express themselves. A good communicator speaks up but also yields the floor to someone else who wants to speak. Being assertive does not mean that you monopolize the discussion.

Be Courteous

There are often as many opinions as there are people in a group. So it is important, when you express an opinion, to speak tactfully. Even when you think someone else is wrong, you should acknowledge others' right to their opinions before you express your own ideas.

Making a Presentation

When you make a presentation, you are the featured speaker and your listeners are your audience. People who are normally relaxed and open when communicating may experience great anxiety when making a presentation. A person who makes effective presentations, however, has learned to project the same personality on stage as in one-to-one conversations.

It's normal to feel anxious about making presentations. However, you can minimize your anxiety by following several basic suggestions for making a good presentation. You can prepare your presentation in advance, relate to your audience, and be yourself.

Prepare Your Presentation

The most effective speakers are prepared. No matter what the subject or the audience, effective presenters have planned their presentations in advance. They know what information they want to communicate and how they will deliver it. Effective presenters follow these basic steps when preparing presentations.

1. Think about the audience and the setting. Is the audience young or old, experienced or inexperienced, male or female? Is the setting formal or informal? The answers to these questions will help you tailor your presentation.
2. Outline your message. Think about your objective and include only information that supports your objective. Remember, people can't absorb too much information at once, so keep the presentation simple. Three or fewer main points are usually enough.
3. Prepare supporting materials. You can reinforce the impact of your message by preparing audio or visual material that supports your message. Presentation software packages like Powerpoint make it easy to produce professional-quality supporting materials on a computer.
4. Rehearse. Run through your presentation a few times. Then find an audience, even if it's only one person. Give your presentation and ask for feedback.

Relate to Your Audience

Presenters who rely primarily on the weight of facts and figures to engage their audiences usually fail. That's because people relate to speakers who relate to them. A good speaker gives a presentation that is relevant and meaningful to the audience, in terms of both its message and how the message is delivered.

Do You Speak Up?

Purpose: Knowing how often you actually engage in speaking with others at key moments helps you to understand the effectiveness of your speaking.

Spend a day keeping track of the number of groups you interact with and the number of times, if any, you speak in each group situation. You can record this information in the chart below.

Description of Group	Number of Times You Spoke

Once you've recorded a day's participation in groups, answer the following questions:

1. Did you speak in each group of which you were a part?

_____

If not, why not?

_____

_____

_____

_____

2. Did you find it easier to speak up in some groups than in others?

_____

If yes, why?

_____

_____

_____

_____

If you have considered your audience and setting before you prepare your presentation, the chances are your message will be meaningful to your listeners. For example, suppose you are giving a talk on the latest browser software. Is your audience made up of experienced computer programmers or people who use computers as appliances? Your presentation will be very different to each of these audiences.

Your presentation will also be more effective if you can relate to your audience in the way you deliver your message. Address yourself to the audience. Talk to them rather than at them. Get them to participate by asking questions, recalling well-known events or people, and having them use their imaginations. If the group is small, the audience can actively participate. If the group is large, you can persuade them as they participate silently.

Be Yourself

Truly effective presenters take these suggestions one step further by communicating something of themselves as individuals. They take off the formal mask and let people see the real person beneath. To be an effective presenter, you must be willing to be open and disclose parts of yourself to the audience.

ELEMENTS OF EXCELLENCE

After reading this chapter, you have learned

> what speech qualities you need to consider when developing your speaking skills.
> about skills that will improve your speaking skills through preparation and practice.
> why the telephone creates challenges to getting your message across.
> how to overcome the jitters that come with public speaking and presentations.

The Information Highway

Getting Up to Speed

There are many Internet Web sites related to speaking skills. Here are a few to get you started.

> **http://bartleby.com.** The Columbia Guide to Standard American English is a reference work available on Bartleby.com.
> **http://www.americandialect.org.** If you are interested in learning more about American dialects, including Black English, visit the Web site of the American Dialect Society.
> **http://www.eslcafe.com.** Dave's ESL Café on the Web is a comprehensive site of interest to speakers of English as a second language. Their search engine provides links to ESL resources on the Internet, including speaking skills resources.
> **http://www.toastmasters.org.** Toastmasters, a worldwide organization dedicated to improving oral presentation skills, has a Web site with information on speaking to groups.

In addition, you can search using key words such as *speaking skills, standard English, Ebonics, American English dialects, English as a second language, voice training, bilingualism* (or a specific language), and *oral presentation.*

JOURNAL

Answer the following journal questions.

1. If you could hire a dialect coach, what aspect of your speech would you change or improve? How would this change in speech benefit you?

_____

_____

_____

_____

_____

_____

_____

_____

2. Describe someone you know who is a good conversationalist. What makes this person so skillful?

_____

_____

_____

_____

_____

_____

_____

_____

3. What role does the telephone play in your life? If you use a cell phone, how has it changed your behavior?

_____

_____

_____

_____

_____

_____

_____

_____

_____

_____

4. In polls, fear of making a speech ranks high, along with fear of snakes. If you get very anxious before you have to speak in public, what can you do to reduce the stress you feel? Given what you have learned in the chapter, what strategies might you try in the future?

_____

_____

_____

_____

_____

_____

_____

_____

_____

_____

_____

Chapter 8

The Power of Personal Interactions

Have you ever watched actors, directors, and other movie people accept an Oscar for their work? Nine times out of ten, Oscar winners thank the people—parents, spouses, friends, or colleagues—who made it possible for them to succeed. People who lead full, successful lives have a tremendous respect for and appreciation of others. They understand that good relationships with the people around them are important to their well-being. People who reach their potential are able to form and maintain good relationships with family, friends, coworkers, customers, and neighbors.

> If you don't look out for others, who will look out for you?
>
> WHOOPI GOLDBERG, ACTRESS

When people start working, they find that it's no longer possible to associate only with people they like. Instead, they are expected to get along with all sorts of people, whether they like them or not. You may be surprised to learn that most people who are dismissed from their jobs are not fired because they can't handle

On the International Space Station, diverse groups of people work together in close quarters for long periods. There's nowhere to go when conflict arises, so astronauts have to learn to resolve their problems and get along.

Trust you? Sure I trust you!
(I wonder what he's after now.)
Be open with you? Of course
I'm open with you! (I'm as open
as I can be with a guy like you.)
Level with you? You know I level
with you! (I'd like to more, but
you can't take it.) Accept you?
Naturally I accept you—like you
do me. (And when you learn to
accept me, I might accept you
more.) What's the hang-up?
What could ever hang up two
open, trusting, leveling, and
accepting guys like us?

LYMAN K. RANDALL

the work. Rather, they are dismissed because they can't get along with colleagues and customers.

In this chapter, you will learn that having positive, effective relationships with the people around you means striking a balance between your needs and their needs. It means committing yourself to ethical values. You will learn what's important to you, what's important to other people, and how you relate to others. You will discover how to give and get feedback from the people around you. And you will learn to handle conflict and anger in a productive way.

Begin with Yourself

What kind of person are you? How do other people see you? Your values, attitudes, beliefs, and emotions are the foundation of your uniqueness. How you act upon these states of mind determines how other people react to you.

Self-Belief

As you recall, people with good self-belief are convinced of their own worth. They believe in their ability to influence events, and they approach new people and new challenges with self-confidence. When you believe in yourself, it's easy to believe in others. You recognize that other people are as important and unique as you are. The inner confidence of self-belief means that you don't feel threatened by everyone around you.

Trust, Respect, and Empathy

Whether you get along well with people depends on you. A good relationship with another person is built on the values of trust, respect, and empathy.

> ➤ Trust means that you can rely on someone else, and he or she can rely on you.

> Respect means that you value the other person, and he or she values you.
> Empathy means you can experience another person's feelings or ideas as if they were your own.

When there is trust, respect, and empathy between two people, there is rapport. Rapport is the essence of good human relations. Good communication can establish and improve the rapport between two people, and poor communication can just as easily break down rapport. People who value trust, respect, and empathy are careful communicators. They avoid sarcastic, accusing, and demeaning comments that may destroy rapport.

Assertiveness

Trust, respect, and empathy show a concern for the feelings and rights of others. Assertiveness shows that you understand the importance of your own feelings and rights as well. Let's suppose, for example, that someone asks you to chair a fund-raising committee for a neighborhood group. You really don't feel comfortable asking for money, and you have no time to spare. If you are passive, you will agree to chair the committee even though it will be an uncomfortable and inconvenient chore. If you are aggressive, you'll shout that you have too much to do to deal with such nonsense. You'll be standing up for your rights but trampling on the feelings of others. If you are assertive, you will refuse the assignment politely.

> Precision of communication is important . . . in our era of hair-trigger balances when a false or misunderstood word may create as much disorder as a sudden thoughtless act.
>
> JAMES THURBER,
> AMERICAN HUMORIST

Framing an Assertive Communication

How can you be assertive and tell people no or disagree with them—and still be polite? You can try framing your response as a three-part communication using these key phrases: (1) I feel, (2) I want, and (3) I will. Here is an example: "I feel uncomfortable asking people for money, but I want to support your efforts even though I don't have time to spare. I will be glad to help on a different committee later in the year." Notice that this response focuses on the speaker's thoughts and feelings but also shows trust, empathy, and respect for the receiver. It gives as much due to the speaker's feelings as to the receiver's needs.

Achieving a Balance between Passivity and Aggression

Achieving a good balance between your own needs and those of others is hard for many people to do. For some people, the problem is not being assertive enough. They feel they are not important enough, or they don't have rights, or their feelings don't matter. The truth is that being passive often leads to resentment and unhappiness. Failing to acknowledge that you have important rights and feelings means you're shortchanging yourself. In these situations, others win, but you lose.

Other people have trouble distinguishing assertive behavior from aggressive behavior. They assert themselves in such a hostile, angry way that they create problems for themselves. Aggressive people tend to alienate those around them. In these situations, everyone loses.

Assertiveness is somewhere between passivity and aggression. It takes thought and practice to be assertive. When you are assertive, you share your feelings in a clear, positive, and courteous way. You are not so polite that people misunderstand your message, and you're not so rude that people feel attacked. In these situations, you win, but others win, too.

Assertiveness is a skill that can be learned. Many companies think it is such an important interpersonal skill that they give employees training in assertiveness techniques.   •

The Fine Line between Assertiveness and Aggression

Purpose: This exercise will assist you with understanding when you are likely to react assertively or aggressively.

Think for a moment about a situation in which you reacted passively and found yourself doing something you really didn't want to do, or in which you reacted aggressively and found yourself involved in an argument.

1. What was the situation?

_____

_____

_____

2. How did you react?

_____

_____

_____

3. What do you think you could have done to protect your rights and feelings without harming the other person?

_____

_____

_____

4. Reframe your response using the "I feel, I want, I will" model.

_____

_____

_____

Consider Your Ethical Values

Many of the values you hold are shared by society in general, and much behavior that our society views as wrong is also against the law. If people break the law, they are punished. Stealing, for example, is both unethical and illegal.

But people also have beliefs about what is right and what is wrong that are not dealt with by the law. For example, lying is unethical, but it is not usually illegal. If you value honesty, you don't lie, your conscience is clear, and you feel comfortable with yourself.

Each of us has a set of ethical values by which we try to live. You may value honesty, trustworthiness, and loyalty, for example. You do your best to behave in a way that reflects these values, and your ethical conduct becomes part of your character.

Employers have expectations about the ethical conduct of students and employees. In a work situation, employers expect workers to put in an honest day's work in return for their pay. Beyond that basic contract, employers expect

> Watch your thoughts; they become words.
> Watch your words; they become actions.
> Watch your actions; they become habits.
> Watch your habits; they become character.
> Watch your character; it becomes your destiny.
>
> FRANK OUTLAW, ACTOR

employees to behave honestly in the dozens of day-to-day situations that arise in the workplace. Taking merchandise home, stealing supplies, using the telephone for personal or long-distance calls, and using a company computer to surf the Internet are examples of unethical behavior.

When it comes to ethical issues, you can behave according to your values fairly easily when the situation involves only yourself. For example, you can easily refrain from taking office supplies home with you. But your sense of what's right may not be the same as your friend's or your boss's. In fact, most people don't give much thought to questions of right and wrong until there is a conflict between their values and other people's values. When an ethical conflict involving others arises, you must decide what to do.

When you have an ethical problem that involves others, think about the situation. Before doing anything, ask yourself what effect your action will have on others and on yourself. It sometimes takes courage to stand up for what you believe is right.

Reach Out to Others

The key to getting along with other people is to treat them with the same courtesy and respect with which you would like to be treated. Of course, doing this is not always easy. For example, people often have difficulty communicating with people of other races or ethnic backgrounds. The meanings people attach to the use of language, facial expressions, and gestures differ from culture to culture, and misunderstandings may be frequent. To overcome cultural barriers, it's important to be open to different ways of life and to communicate carefully. Don't assume you have been understood completely, and don't assume you have understood the other person completely, either.

While acknowledging that each person is different, keep in mind that people have many things in common. There are basic hopes, fears, and emotions that we all experience. Understanding these human feelings and empathizing with others form the basis for good relationships with people. Take the risk to ask about what you and the person you are communicating with have in common.

What Do People Need?

The quality of empathy is the basis for good human relations skills. Being able to imagine what another person feels, thinks, and needs means that you are able to interact with him or her in an intelligent and caring way. And when people sense that you are attuned to their needs, they react positively to you.

In the course of a day, you may encounter many people, all of them unique, with whom you must interact in a positive way. How can you make sense of the bewildering variety of emotions, thoughts, feelings, and needs of each person you meet? You may find it helpful to think of people's needs in terms of a hierarchy, as shown in Figure 8-1. Abraham Maslow, a psychologist,

Figure 8-1: Maslow's hierarchy of needs provides a way to think about human needs. In general, people try to satisfy lower-level needs before higher-level needs.

Self-actualization needs

Esteem needs

Love and belonging needs

Safety and security needs

Physiological needs: hunger and thirst

proposed that people are motivated by different levels of needs depending on their circumstances. Homeless people, for example, have basic survival needs: They must find food or starve. Once hunger is satisfied, they can attend to their personal safety. If security needs are satisfied, people can think about meeting the need for love and relationships with others. Once feeling secure in their ties to others, people can focus on meeting their needs for achievement, competence, and self-respect.

When people feel healthy, safe, loved, and competent, they can pursue the highest level of needs—what Maslow called self-actualization (and what we have been calling "reaching your potential"). Self-actualization is reached when people are fulfilled in every aspect of their being. Not many of us experience complete and lasting self-actualization. Occasionally, we may have peak experiences in which we feel moments of perfect happiness or fulfillment. These feelings might come from creating a work of art, falling in love, running a race, or having a baby. Unfortunately, the peak experiences do not last long.

Maslow did not view his hierarchy of needs as rigid. In other words, people do not always focus on their needs in sequential order. They sometimes focus on higher-level needs even when lower-level needs remain only partly fulfilled. Parents, for example, may neglect their own needs to give loved children something extra, or good Samaritans may neglect their need for personal safety to come to the aid of someone in trouble. Even though people may not always attend to their needs in hierarchial order, Maslow's model is helpful when you're trying to figure out a person's motivations. It's also helpful to use the model when you are setting goals.

How Do You Relate to Others?

Another way of thinking about human relations is to focus on the dynamics of the relationship itself, rather than on your needs or the needs of the other person. When you first meet someone, you tend to be cautious and guarded about revealing yourself. As you reveal more about yourself to the other person, trust and empathy develop. The other person also lets her or his guard down and reveals more to you. Gradually, the relationship deepens and becomes more intimate. The quality of a relationship depends on the degree of mutual trust and openness.

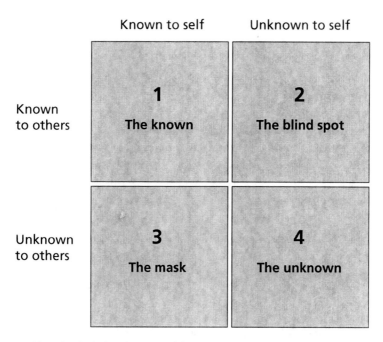

	Known to self	Unknown to self
Known to others	**1** The known	**2** The blind spot
Unknown to others	**3** The mask	**4** The unknown

Figure 8-2: The Johari window is a way of diagramming the amount of shared and unshared knowledge in a relationship. The more shared knowledge there is between people (Box 1), the more openness and trust in the relationship.

The Johari Window

One way of diagramming the effect of mutual understanding and knowledge on a relationship is to use the Johari window (see Figure 8-2). The Johari window is named after its inventors, Joseph Luft and Harry Ingham. It is a square with four sections, each section representing information known or unknown to yourself and to others.

The Known. The first section of the Johari window represents the part of the relationship characterized by openness, shared information, and mutual understanding. In this section are matters known to yourself and to the other person as well. The more intimate and productive the relationship, the larger this section grows. If you sketched a Johari window representing your relationship with a close friend, this section would be large. It might be small, however, if you sketched your relationship with an instructor or manager. If you are shy, this section might be small in most of your relationships.

The Blind Spot. The second section of the Johari window consists of feelings, behaviors, and information that is known to the other person but not to you. This section is sometimes called the blind spot. The unknown matters may include your annoying mannerisms (of which you are unaware) or the other person's hidden motivations. Whatever is unknown to you in the relationship is a handicap. Therefore, the larger this section, the less effective you are in the relationship.

PITFALLS

The challenge of the blind spot is worth additional and serious note. Your blind spot is potentially what will keep you from moving to the next level in your career, and can keep you from building effective relationships with friends and partners. Take the time to ask others what they see as your blind spots . . . and be open to their feedback. You may learn that areas that you thought were most attractive to others are actually keeping you from getting closer.

The Mask. The third section of the Johari window also limits your effectiveness in a relationship, but in a different way. It is everything that you know but the other person doesn't. This information, unknown to the other person, provides you with a protective mask. At first glance, it might seem that the more you know that the other person doesn't, the better off you are. If power is your object, this may be true. But if the mask becomes so large that it crowds out openness (the first section of the Johari window), the relationship suffers from a lack of trust and rapport. So, for example, if you are asked to show a coworker how to do something, and you withhold critical information, the coworker may fail and you may look competent. But in the long run, you have set the tone for a relationship in which there is little trust or cooperation.

The Unknown. The fourth section of the Johari window consists of matters that are unknown to both people. These matters include information about the context of the relationship, each person's psychological makeup, personality traits, creative potential, and so on. As a relationship develops, the size of this section of the Johari window may decrease.

Using the Johari Window to Improve Relationships

As you may have realized, the four sections of the Johari window are not fixed in size. As a relationship develops and changes, the internal vertical and horizontal lines, which separate the known from the unknown, can move. In other words, you can take actions that will increase the size of the first section, the known, to make a more effective relationship. By being open, trusting, and sharing information, you can decrease the size of your mask (section 3).

You can also increase the size of the first section, the known, by decreasing your blind spot. One way to do this is through honest introspection. That is, you must examine your feelings and behavior to understand your needs and motivations. Another way to decrease your blind spot is to ask another person for feedback. What information does the other person have that will help you in the relationship? Using feedback to decrease your blind spot requires the cooperation of the other person. And the amount of cooperation you get will depend in part on your own willingness to be open and to share.

Feedback in Relationships

Giving and getting feedback makes relationships grow and develop. Whether the growth is healthy or stunted depends in large part on our ability to give feedback in a nonthreatening way and to receive feedback without being crushed by it. Of course, some feedback is positive. Praise and affirmation are good to give and to receive, and most of us thrive on them. Dealing with negative feedback is much more difficult.

Diagram Two Relationships

Purpose: The Johari window gives poignant insight as to how our relationships with people can give us information about ourselves and how we value relationships. Use the Johari windows below to diagram two relationships. Use the first window to model a relationship with a spouse, lover, or friend. Use the second window to model a relationship with a fellow student, coworker, or acquaintance.

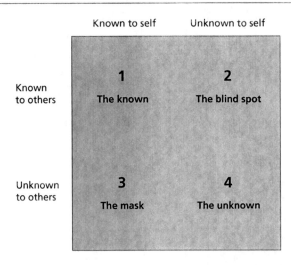

Giving Feedback

Feedback is part of a communication loop that helps create the knowledge, openness, and mutual trust necessary for effective relationships. As we saw from the Johari window, the larger the area of mutual knowledge, the more effective the relationship. Giving feedback is one way to increase what is known about a relationship.

It takes skill to give negative feedback in a way that helps the other person. The person who is being helped must feel respected and valued, not demeaned. So it's important when giving feedback to be calm, concerned, and encouraging. You must accept the other person without judging him or her, and direct the criticism at behaviors, not at personality. For example, if parents criticize children's behavior by telling them they are bad, the children feel demeaned and worthless. If, on the other hand, parents give specific feedback about behavior—such as it's rude to interrupt—the children's self-esteem is intact and they have some idea how to behave in the future.

When you give feedback in a relationship, keep these things in mind:

> Understand your own feelings and motivations.
> Be accepting and nonjudgmental about the other person.
> Be sensitive to the other person's resistance. Pressure doesn't work in the long run.
> Criticize specific behavior, not personality.
> Give feedback only on matters that the other person can change. If something can't be changed, there's little value in discussing it.
> Don't tell others what to do.

Receiving Feedback

Even harder than giving productive criticism is being on the receiving end of negative feedback. Our first reaction to criticism is often defensive. Rather than being open to the criticism, we react by protecting our self-belief.

News & Views

Who Do You Think You Are? It Depends . . .

Your cultural background influences every aspect of your life. Some of these influences are very apparent—for example, the holidays you celebrate. But other influences are harder to see because they involve the way you think about yourself and relate to others. One example of culture influencing the way people think and behave is the idea of the self.

Some cultures define the self primarily as an individual. In these cultures, the individual is thought of as being an independent entity. The individual is emotionally separate from groups, including family groups. Individual-centered cultures place a high value on self-reliance and competitiveness. Does this sound familiar? It should, because mainstream culture in the United States is individual-centered.

Other cultures define the self in relation to a group. In these cultures, the individual's core identity is closely embedded in that of the group. These cultures place a high value on solidarity, concern for others, and cooperation. Group-centered cultures include those of Japan and other East Asian nations, as well as Mexico and other Latin American countries.

People from an individual-centered culture like that of the United States see themselves as independent, with clear boundaries between themselves and others. People from a group-centered culture like those of Japan or China see themselves as interdependent with others.

You can see that the way you think of yourself influences how you relate to others. Keep these ideas of the self in mind when you are thinking about your relationship with others, especially those whose view of the self may differ from yours. (Adapted from Hazel R. Markus and Shinobu Kitayama, "Culture and the Self," *Psychological Review,* vol. 98, no. 2, 1991, p. 226.)

Source: Bruce Bower, "Western Notions of the Mind May Not Translate to Other Cultures," *Science News,* vol. 152, October 18, 1997, p. 248ff.; Gina M. Shkodriani and Judith L. Gibbons, "Individualism and Collectivism among University Students in Mexico and the United States," *Journal of Social Psychology,* vol. 135, December 1995, p. 765ff.

Protecting Your Self-Belief

Our self-belief is so important to our well-being that people have evolved many ways to defend it. These processes, which reduce anxiety and protect our self-belief, are called defense mechanisms. Some common defense mechanisms are withdrawal, rationalization, substitution, fantasy, and projection. The defense mechanisms are not unhealthy unless they come to dominate our interactions with others.

Withdrawal. People who feel threatened sometimes deal with their anxiety by trying to avoid the situation that caused the stress. Trying to escape from negative feedback is called withdrawal. People who have difficulty with the give and take of close relationships often withdraw. Separation, divorce, quitting a job—all may be examples of withdrawal.

Rationalization. Another way to defend your self-belief is to rationalize, that is, to explain or excuse an unacceptable situation in terms that make it acceptable to yourself. Rationalizing involves distorting the truth to make it more acceptable. For example, if you are criticized for forgetting an important customer at work, you may rationalize that it was your boss's responsibility to remind you, whereas in truth it was your responsibility.

> In the right key one can say anything. In the wrong key, nothing: the only delicate part is the establishment of the key.
> GEORGE BERNARD SHAW, IRISH PLAYWRIGHT AND CRITIC

Displacement. Displacement is a defense mechanism in which you react to a negative situation by substituting another person for the person who aroused your anxiety or anger. For example, if your instructor criticizes you in front of the class, you may go home and yell at your sister. In general, the person you choose as the substitute is less likely to harm your self-belief.

Fantasy. Fantasy is a form of withdrawal in which daydreams provide a boost to self-belief when reality threatens. For example, if you've been told that you'll be off the team unless your work improves, you may fantasize about being indispensable to your work group and leading it to success. Everyone fantasizes to a degree; fantasy becomes a problem only when it is a substitute for reality.

Projection. Projection is a defense mechanism in which you attribute your own unacceptable behaviors and feelings to another person. If you are criticized for treating a coworker discourteously, for example, you may project that the coworker was being rude to you.

Handling Feedback Positively

All the defense mechanisms can help us maintain our self-belief. But at what cost? People who are always on the defensive find it hard to change and grow. Their relationships with others are characterized by a lack of openness and trust. On the other hand, people who can handle negative feedback constructively have an opportunity to develop and grow. Their relationships with others become more, not less, effective.

How can you handle negative feedback in a positive way? Learning to accept feedback means paying less attention to how criticism makes you feel and more attention to what's actually being said. If you remember that criticism is information that can help you, you will be able to deal with it more effectively. Try these tips for handling negative feedback.

> Consider who is criticizing you. Is the person in a position to know what he or she is talking about? If not, the criticism may not be valid. If so, it's worth listening to.
> Is the person criticizing you upset about something else? If so, he or she may just be blowing off steam. If he or she is calm, though, you should pay more attention.
> Ask for specific information. Many people who offer criticism do so in the most general terms, which is not helpful.
> Think about what you've heard. Give yourself time to react.
> Decide whether the criticism is appropriate. If it is, think about what you will do to change your behavior.

Conflict

> Anybody can become angry—that is easy; but to be angry with the right person, and to the right degree, and at the right time, and for the right purpose, and in the right way—that is not within everybody's power and is not easy.
>
> ARISTOTLE, ANCIENT GREEK PHILOSOPHER

Throw any two people together for any length of time and they are sure to disagree about something. The conflict may be over what time they go to the movies or whether war can be morally justified. If they cannot settle the disagreement, they may become frustrated and angry. This scenario is so common that you may think conflict is always a negative experience. Yet if handled properly, conflict can have healthy and productive results.

What Causes Conflict?

Differences over facts, ideas, goals, needs, attitudes, beliefs, and personalities all cause conflict. Some conflicts are simple and easy to resolve. A difference of opinion about a fact, for example, usually does not escalate into an emotional battle.

But conflicts about personalities, values, needs, beliefs, and ideas can be more serious. Such conflicts often cause frustration and anger. The issues are more fundamental, and they can have an emotional component that makes disagreement threatening. Unless the anger is dealt with properly, the conflict is not resolved. In addition, when people feel that the outcome of a conflict is a reflection of their self-belief, conflict can be damaging.

Anger

Anger, the result of unresolved conflict, is a powerful emotion. Think about the last time you got angry. What did you do? Did you tell the other person why you were angry? Did you snap at them about something else? Or did you keep your feelings to yourself? People express anger in different ways.

Expressing Anger Directly

People often express their anger directly. If someone annoys you, you tell them so, or you glare at them, or you shove them, or you tailgate them on the road. Obviously, the direct expression of anger can run the gamut from assertiveness to aggression to violence. How people express anger directly depends on their personalities and the extent to which they are provoked. People with negative self-belief often have an underlying attitude of hostility that is easily triggered by even minor events. Others, more secure in their self-belief, can express anger more calmly without being aggressive.

Expressing Anger Indirectly

Another way to express anger is indirect. Instead of confronting the person with whom you are angry, you direct your anger at a third party, who is less threatening. Since this process is similar to the defense mechanism of dis-placement, it is often called displacement.

In many situations it is inappropriate to express anger at the person with whom you are angry. Suppose you've just started your own business and one of your clients keeps changing his mind about what he wants you to do. You are angry, because he's wasting your time. Yet expressing anger directly will cause you to lose a customer. In this case your anger may find an outlet when you snap at your child or a friend.

Internalizing Anger

The third way to deal with anger is to keep it bottled up inside you. Many people consider the expression of anger to be threatening, bad, or rude, and so they internalize it. Unfortunately, the result of internalizing anger is that you feel a growing resentment. Since your anger is not expressed, there is no way for the conflict to be resolved, and it festers.

Controlling Anger

You can minimize the destructiveness of anger by trying to control it. There are several approaches that you can take.

> Don't say or do anything immediately. It's usually best to cool off and give yourself a chance to think. Counting to 10 may help.
> Figure out why you are angry. Sometimes the cause of the anger is something you can easily change or avoid.
> Channel your anger into physical exercise. Even a walk can relieve the tensions of anger.
> Use relaxation techniques such as deep breathing to calm yourself.
> Find a friend who will listen and offer constructive suggestions.

Resolving Conflicts

Once your anger is under control, you can try to resolve the conflict that caused it. The energy created by your anger can be channeled into solving the problem. Here are a few suggestions.

It is hidden wrath that harms.

SENECA, ANCIENT
ROMAN PHILOSOPHER,
DRAMATIST, AND
STATESMAN

> Commit yourself to resolving the problem that caused the conflict. Don't just decide to keep the peace.
> Ask yourself what you hope to achieve by resolving the conflict. Is it critical to get your way, or is your relationship with the other person more important? Your priorities will influence how you settle the conflict.
> Make sure you and the other person have the same understanding of the reason for conflict. Ask questions and really listen. You may be surprised: Some conflicts are the result of misunderstanding.
> Be assertive, not aggressive. Remember that the other person has rights and feelings, too.
> Try to keep to the facts. When discussing the issue, make sure you understand the difference between facts and feelings. The more you can keep feelings out of it, the better your chance for resolving the conflict.

Take an Anger Inventory

Some people get angry easily, and others remain calm. Where are you in this spectrum? This exercise will help you to understand how anger impacts your daily interactions.

Raymond W. Novaco of the University of California devised an anger inventory on which the following questionnaire is based. For each item, indicate whether you would be very angry, somewhat angry, or not angry by circling the numbers 1, 2, or 3.

	Very Angry	Somewhat Angry	Not Angry
1. Your coworker makes a mistake and blames it on you.	1	2	3
2. You are talking to a friend, and she doesn't answer.	1	2	3
3. You lose a game.	1	2	3
4. An acquaintance always brags about himself.	1	2	3
5. Your boss tells you your work is poor.	1	2	3
6. You are driving on a highway and someone cuts in front of you.	1	2	3
7. At a store, a salesperson keeps following you and offering help.	1	2	3
8. A car drives through a puddle and splashes you.	1	2	3
9. Someone turns off the TV while you are watching a program.	1	2	3
10. You are studying and someone is tapping his fingers.	1	2	3

Add the numbers you circled in each column. Then add the subtotals to get your grand total.

Grand Total: _____

If your score was:

10–15 You get angry quickly.
16–20 You get angry fairly easily.
21–25 You have a moderate level of anger.
26–30 You are slow to get angry.

Whatever It Takes

Colin Powell

Colin Powell's story is an American classic. The son of immigrants from Jamaica, Powell grew up in the South Bronx. He attended New York City public schools. Even though Powell was not an enthusiastic student, his parents made him do his homework every day and do his best. As a result, says Powell, "I got a pretty good education."

Colin Powell was an average student in college, too. Indeed, what interested him most was the ROTC military program he joined at the City College of New York. "The discipline, the structure, the camaraderie, the sense of belonging were what I craved," said Powell. After graduation with a degree in geology, Powell joined the army.

Powell's career as a soldier spanned 35 years. He began as a junior lieutenant and retired as a four-star general. During his years with the army, he had many jobs ranging from battalion commander in Korea to chairman of the Joint Chiefs of Staff, the highest-ranking position in the armed services. Powell was the first African American and the youngest man ever to be appointed to that position, which he held during the Persian Gulf War in the early 1990s.

After his retirement from the military, Powell twice had the opportunity to run for president. Both times he declined, indicating that he didn't have the necessary passion to be a politician. In 2001 President George W. Bush appointed Powell secretary of state, the first African American to hold this position. As secretary of state, Powell's job was to accomplish U.S. foreign policy goals through diplomacy.

With so much experience of war, Powell understands how terrible violence is. "Soldiers know what it's like to be scared in battle—that's why soldiers hate war and try to avoid violence," Powell said in an interview with students. "Always try to avoid violence, to avoid fighting. Try to solve problems by respecting each other and by talking to each other."

Sources: "Biography: Colin L. Powell, Secretary of State," U.S. Department of State, http://www.state.gov/r/pa/ei/biog/1349.htm; "Colin L. Powell," Thomson-Gale, http://www.galegroup.com/free_resources/bhm/bio/powell_c.htm; "General Colin Powell: Symbol of Integrity Walks Moderate Path," ABC News, http://abcnews.go.com/sections/politics/DailyNews/profile_powell.html; "Meet General Colin L. Powell: Interview Transcript," Scholastic, http://teacher/scholastic.com/barrier/powellchat/transcript.htm; all accessed March 13, 2003.

At first, you may find it difficult to control your anger and to approach conflicts in a more thoughtful, rational way. With practice, you will become more comfortable in dealing with conflict. You may find that effectively resolving conflict is a way to learn more about yourself and to grow, as well as to improve the quality of your relationships with the people around you.

> A soft answer turneth away wrath; but grievous words stir up anger.
>
> PROVERBS 15:1 BIBLE

ELEMENTS OF EXCELLENCE

After reading this chapter, you have learned

> ➤ how your personal values impact your ability to interrelate with others effectively.
> ➤ what others need to feel important and what you can do to reach out to them.
> ➤ how using the Johari window can teach you about your relationships and your role in them.
> ➤ why understanding how to give and receive feedback will improve your relationships.
> ➤ how to react to and effectively manage conflict.

Getting Up to Speed

Some Web sites related to the topics covered in this chapter include the following.

> ➤ **http://www.queendom.com.** You can take an inventory to see how assertive you are at a site that focuses on women's health issues (men can take the inventory, too).
> ➤ **http://www.ethicsweb.ca.** Ethics Web maintains a site that provides links to ethics resources on the Internet, including links to business ethics.
> ➤ **http://www.drdriving.org.** You can find tips on how to deal with aggression on the road, known as road rage, from "Dr. Driving."
> ➤ **http://www.acrnet.org.** If you are interested in different approaches to conflict resolution, check the Web site of the Association for Conflict Resolution.

In addition, you will find thousands of possible sites by using a search engine and entering the key words *assertiveness, aggression, road rage, ethics, interpersonal relationships,* and *conflict resolution.*

JOURNAL

Answer the following journal questions.

1. How good are you at getting along with others? What aspects of your relationships with others would you like to improve?

_____

_____

_____

_____

_____

_____

_____

2. Explain your code of ethics. What ethical values are most important to you? Least important? Why?

_____

_____

_____

_____

_____

_____

_____

_____

3. Describe the most successful relationship in your life. What makes this relationship work? How can you improve it?

_____

_____

_____

_____

_____

_____

_____

_____

4. Describe a conflict you've recently experienced. How was the conflict resolved? In your view, was the resolution successful? Explain.

_____

_____

_____

_____

_____

_____

_____

Chapter 9

Functioning in Groups

From the time you were born into a family until this moment, when you are reading these words for a class, you have belonged to hundreds of groups. Psychologists define a group as the conscious interaction of two or more people. This means that the members of a group must be aware of one another. So, for example, people shopping at J.C. Penney are not a group unless an incident takes place that makes them pay attention to one another. If a security guard starts chasing a shoplifter and people stop to watch, they become members of a group.

> Man is a social animal.
>
> SENECA, ANCIENT ROMAN PHILOSOPHER, DRAMATIST, AND STATESMAN

The group at J.C. Penney lasts just a few minutes and breaks up. Other groups, such as the U.S. Senate or the Dave Matthews Band, last for years. And some groups, like the one in the department store, are informal. Informal groups are loose associations of people without stated rules. Passengers on a bus, a group of friends, or people at a party are all part of informal groups. Other groups are formal; that is, they have clear goals and established rules. Political parties, businesses, educational affiliations, labor unions, orchestras, baseball teams, and other such associations are all formal groups.

©KEVIN FLEMING/CORBIS

One of the purposes of basic training is to forge group bonds. As soldiers gain more experience, some will demonstrate leadership skills and be promoted up the ranks.

Group Dynamics

Group dynamics is the study of how people interact in groups. All groups have goals they try to achieve; roles for members to play; norms, or standards of behavior; communication patterns; and a degree of cohesiveness.

Goals

All groups have goals, whether they are explicitly stated or taken for granted, short-term or long-term. People at a party, for example, are there to have a good time. A business's goal may be to make a profit by serving a particular market. A hockey team's goal is to win as many games as possible.

In groups, the goals can be cooperative or competitive. When the goals are cooperative, people in the group work together to achieve an objective. A group putting on a play, for example, has a cooperative goal. When group goals are competitive, people in the group work against one another to achieve their objectives. Four people playing Monopoly have competitive goals; only one can win the game.

Of course, in real life things are seldom so clear-cut. In most groups, there are both cooperative and competitive goals at the same time. Take the example of a theater group: Clearly, the cooperative goal is to have the play ready to perform on opening night. Yet the actors in the group may have competitive goals. Each may be trying to win the most applause or the best reviews.

Most of the groups you will encounter, both at home and at work, will have both cooperative and competitive goals. Today, for example, many businesses organize their workers into project teams. Members of the team cooperate with one another to achieve the goals of the team. At the same time they compete with other teams in the organization. They may even compete with each other. Consider a corporation that creates teams of workers to develop new products. People on the widget team cooperate with one another to design, produce, and market the best and most profitable widget. At the same time, they compete with people on the gadget team, who are trying to design, produce, and market the best and most profitable gadget. The widget people are also competing among themselves for recognition, promotion, raises, and power.

Studies have shown that groups with cooperative goals have better communication and are more productive. In groups with competitive goals, members tend to spend too much energy on rivalry. However, competitive goals can be positive forces. They can create a feeling of challenge and excitement that motivates people to do their best.

Roles and Norms

If you pitch for your baseball team, you are expected to stand on the pitcher's mound, try to strike out the opposing batter, catch any fly balls that come your way, and so on. On the team, your role is pitcher, and your norms are the rules of baseball. In a group, a role is a set of expected behaviors for a particular position. Norms are the rules by which people in particular roles are expected to behave.

Norms cover almost all aspects of our interactions with other people, although they vary from one culture to another. For example, when in public, women in many Muslim countries are expected to wear a chador, a cloth that covers the head and veils the face. In the United States, in contrast, most women cover their heads only when it is cold. Norms change gradually over time and through the influence of one culture on another. For example, 50 years ago blue jeans were considered appropriate wear for people who did manual labor or farm work. Today blue jeans are acceptable on a wide range of people in all but the most formal or conservative settings.

There are many roles that have a substantial number of norms associated with them. Mother, father, wife, husband, child, friend, boss, employee, teacher, and student are common roles with dozens of norms. Employees, for example, are expected to be punctual, conscientious, hardworking, and loyal. Friends are expected to be supportive and loyal. The norms for these roles are deeply ingrained in our society, and they help make it function smoothly.

In many formal groups, explicit roles are assigned to members. In a committee a chairperson leads and a secretary records the minutes. In a band, there may be a singer, guitarist, keyboard player, and drummer. In a large business, there are salespeople, marketing staff, research and development staff, engineers, manufacturing workers, and administrative support workers (see Figure 9-1).

In many companies, an employee plays a role in different work teams, not just in his or her department. For example, an engineer may be on the staff of the engineering department. But she may also be on several work teams with people from other departments of the company. The engineer may represent her department on several project work teams with different designers, manufacturing supervisors, and marketing managers. Not only does she need technical engineering skills but also she needs people skills to work well with others on her teams. Be prepared to take on differing roles depending on your setting.

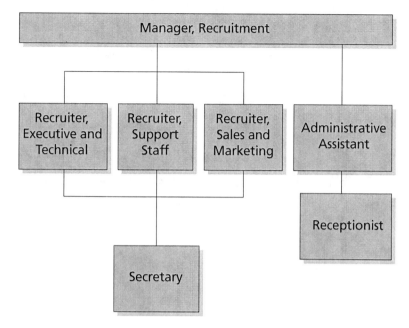

Figure 9-1: An organization chart shows the roles people play in an organization. Here a small part of a corporation's human resources department is shown.

Your Work Environment as a Group

Purpose: This exercise helps you to understand how a current work team that you belong to may be effective or strained. Think about a current work team that you belong to. Then answer the following questions.

1. What are the cooperative goals of the team, if any?

_____

_____

_____

_____

_____

2. What are the competitive goals of the team, if any?

_____

_____

_____

_____

_____

3. What team roles can you identify? What role do you play?

_____

_____

_____

_____

_____

4. What norms do you associate with each role you identify?

_____

_____

_____

_____

_____

_____

Communication

As you participate in groups, observe the communication patterns. Does one person dominate, telling everyone else what to do? Do two or three people talk among themselves while the rest observe? Is communication like a chain, with messages passed from one person to another? Or do all members communicate with all other members?

Communication patterns can tell you a great deal about groups. In formal groups, communication patterns may be rigid. For example, in the armed services, the communication pattern looks like a chain (see Figure 9-2). Messages are passed down the chain from the higher ranks to the lower ranks and

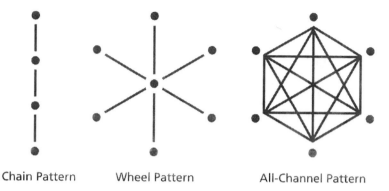

| Chain Pattern | Wheel Pattern | All-Channel Pattern |

Figure 9-2: There are three basic communication patterns in groups: In the chain pattern, a message is passed from one person to the next. In the wheel pattern, the person at the hub communicates with each person on the spokes, but the people on the spokes don't communicate with each other. In the all-channel pattern, all members communicate with each other.

occasionally in the other direction. Skipping a link of the chain is a serious breach of group norms in the armed services.

Another example of a formal communication pattern is called the wheel. One person at the hub communicates with each group member on the spokes, but the members do not communicate with each other. An example of this is a dispatcher directing the activity of a group of electronics service technicians, or an office manager supervising a group of clerks.

In smaller, less formal groups, such as a project team, social group, or small business, members communicate more freely with one another in the all-channel pattern. In theory, each group member communicates with every other group member, although in practice the pattern may be more random.

Cohesiveness

All groups have a certain amount of cohesiveness, that is, the degree to which members stick together. Very cohesive groups have a strong identity and clear goals and norms, and their members are very loyal to one another. Families usually have a high degree of cohesiveness, as do some religious congregations and social groups.

A certain amount of cohesiveness is good; it keeps the group from falling apart and it keeps members cooperating to achieve group goals. One of the jobs of a coach or manager, for example, is to encourage the cohesiveness of the team or department. But too much cohesiveness can cause problems, as we shall see.

Draw a Communication Pattern

Purpose: In this exercise you will visually represent the communication patterns in your life. By doing so, you will gain new insights about both family and work.

In the space below, draw the typical communication pattern of your workplace and your family.

Your Workplace   **Your Family**

How People Behave in Groups

Have you ever found yourself doing something you wouldn't ordinarily do because "everyone else is doing it"? You might have cheated on an exam, gotten your navel pierced, or spent too much money on something fashionable. The cohesiveness of your group caused you to behave in a way that was contrary to your beliefs or values. You found yourself conforming or complying with the group's norms. In some groups this condition goes so far that it has been given a special name, *groupthink*.

Conformity

Changing your opinion or behavior in response to pressure from a group is called conformity. The urge to conform can be extremely powerful, as was shown in a famous experiment conducted by psychologist Solomon Asch. Groups of seven students were told they were participating in an experiment about perception. They were shown these cards and asked to select the line on the right-hand card that matches the line on the left-hand card (see Figure 9-3).

No doubt you picked the correct line without any trouble. But how would you do in the following situation? In Asch's study, six of the seven students were "in" on the true nature of the experiment. The group was given the same task: to match the sticks. The six were instructed to answer unanimously, out loud in front of the group. The seventh, the true subject, answered last, also out loud. At first, the six answered correctly, and so did the true subject. But then the six started to unanimously select the incorrect line, contradicting what the seventh subject could see perfectly well. In one out of three groups, the true subjects conformed—that is, they gave the wrong answer to go along with the group.

In follow-up interviews, it became apparent that both the conformers and the ones who stuck to the evidence of their senses were disturbed by what happened. The conformers reported that their feelings of self-confidence had been eroded by the unanimous judgments of the other group members. Those who remained independent of the group reported feeling embarrassed and uneasy at being the odd one out.

Of course, it's important to realize that conformity is not always bad. In common social situations such as waiting in line, entering an elevator, or taking a class, conformity is simply convenient behavior. It means that these situations will take place in a way that everyone expects. It relieves people of the necessity of making a decision about what to do all day long.

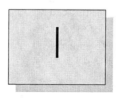 

Figure 9-3: Which of the lines on the right-hand card matches the line on the left-hand card?

Prejudice, Stereotypes, and Discrimination

In 1902 Takuji Yamashita, a Japanese immigrant, graduated from the University of Washington law school. He passed the bar exam with honors, but the State of Washington said that Yamashita could not be a lawyer. At the time, Japanese immigrants could not apply for American citizenship, and a person had to be a citizen in order to be a lawyer. Yamashita argued his own case in court, saying that laws excluding people based on race were unworthy of "the most enlightened and liberty-loving nation of them all." The court agreed that Yamashita was "intellectually and morally" qualified to be a lawyer. However, he lost his case because the prejudices of the time were built into the legal system.

COURTESY OF THE DESCENDANTS OF TAKUJI YAMASHITA

Ninety-nine years later, the laws excluding nonwhites from citizenship were no longer on the books. So in 2001, 42 years after Yamashita's death, the State of Washington finally admitted him to the bar. In a special ceremony attended by his descendants, Yamashita was awarded the honor for which he had studied and fought.

Like all victims of prejudice, Yamashita was prejudged because of his background. Prejudice is a negative attitude about people based on their belonging to a particular group, without any regard for their individuality. Stereotypes are the simplified beliefs that people have about the characteristics of members of a particular group. And discrimination is action taken against someone we are prejudiced against.

Where does prejudice come from? Psychologists have different ideas about the origins of prejudice. Some think that prejudice is the result of competition between groups. When blacks and whites, or Americans and Mexicans, for example, compete for jobs, members of both groups become prejudiced against the other group.

Other psychologists believe that prejudice is learned behavior. In this view, children acquire the prejudices of the adults around them, much as they learn any other type of behavior.

Another theory holds that people with certain personality traits are more likely to be prejudiced. People who are rigid and conventional, and who have poor self-belief, are prone toward prejudice. They feel better about themselves when they can feel better than others.

Still another point of view is that prejudice is a result of lazy thinking. Because the world is so complex and hard to understand, people resort to stereotypes to simplify their thinking and to categorize people.

Most people have prejudices, and most people are either unaware of them or won't admit to them. Prejudice that results in unfair discrimination harms the people discriminated against, like Yamashita. Today legislation makes discrimination based on sex, age, race, ethnicity, or religion illegal. Yet discrimination still persists in the attitudes and behavior of individuals.

Conformity

The important thing about conformity is to know when it is appropriate. In most circumstances, it probably is appropriate. But when the beliefs, values, and behavior of a group run counter to your own beliefs, values, and codes of behavior, then whether to conform becomes an important decision. Do you go along to get along, or do you act independently? This can be a hard question to answer.

Groupthink

When a group is very cohesive and its members very loyal to one another, a special type of conformity sometimes arises. Called groupthink, it is an uncritical acceptance of a group's beliefs and behaviors in order to preserve its unanimity. When loyalty to the group becomes more important than anything else, the members are suffering from groupthink.

> The opinion of the majority is not the final proof of what is right.
>
> FRIEDRICH VON SCHILLER, 18TH-CENTURY GERMAN DRAMATIST, POET, AND HISTORIAN

When a group is suffering from groupthink, its members lose their ability to think critically and independently. They lose sight of their own values and of moral consequences

Participating in Groups

You can use your knowledge about how groups work to improve the way you interact with others. By analyzing the goals, roles, and norms of the groups you belong to, you will be able to understand the nature of each group. You can also get the most out of groups by learning to be an active participant.

Analyzing Group Goals, Roles, and Norms

When you first join a group, are you quiet at first? Do you keep to yourself, observing how people interact? Most people behave this way when they join a new group. Unconsciously, they are trying to understand the group's goals, roles, and norms.

You can sharpen your powers of analysis by asking yourself some questions when you first encounter a group. As you observe, try to answer the following questions:

> What are the objectives of the group?
> Are the group's goals cooperative or competitive?
> Does the group function as a team, or are there rivalries among members?
> Are some members pursuing individual goals rather than group goals?
> Does the group have a leader? Who is the leader?
> What other roles are apparent in the group?
> What are the norms of the group? Is it formal or informal?
> What communication patterns are being used?

By answering these questions, you will better understand the nature of the group and your role in it. As you begin to feel comfortable with the norms of the group, you can start to participate more actively.

Conformity in Your Work Team

Purpose: By completing this exercise, you will have a better understanding of how strong conformity is within your team, and whether groupthink exists.

Think about your work team again, and answer the following questions.

1. Give two examples of conformity in the team.

_____

_____

_____

_____

2. Describe a situation in which a member of the team did not conform to group norms.

_____

_____

_____

_____

_____

_____

3. Does the team suffer from groupthink? Give evidence to support your answer.

_____

_____

_____

_____

_____

_____

Participating Actively

Groups tend to accept those who adopt their norms, and reject those who ignore them. So once you figure out the norms of a group, you will have better success if you behave accordingly. If the group is formal, with rules of order, then you too will have to be formal. If the group is informal, you can behave in a more casual manner.

Whatever It Takes

Mike Krzyzewski

When Mike Krzyzewski arrived at Duke University in 1981 to coach its basketball team, the school newspaper wrote "that is not a typo" next to his name. Krzyzewski, pronounced "sha-shef-ski," thought that was pretty funny. Known as Coach K at Duke, Krzyzewski has built an impressive men's basketball program. Duke's team, the Blue Devils, has won three national championships and has had six national players of the year. In addition, all but two of Coach K's players who played all four years have graduated. Many have gone on to play in the NBA.

What makes Coach K's teams so successful? Krzyzewski has created a special Blue Devils culture that is not focused on winning. Instead, Krzyzewski emphasizes the kids on the team and the coaches who assist him. He values them even when they fail. As a result, the team "tries to play hard for him and tries to play great for him" in the words of a former player.

In 2001, in honor of his coaching achievements, Krzyzewski was inducted into the Basketball Hall of Fame. In his acceptance speech, Krzyzewski said, "I hope that all of those youngsters who have played for me and the people who have worked with me will share in this honor. My mom always told me to associate myself with great people and great institutions, and I have tried to do that."

According to Krzyzewski, the son of Polish immigrants, his mother taught him not to fear losing. "She loved me no matter what happened. I didn't realize how powerful that was until I got older," says Krzyzewski. His parents pressured him to join the armed forces and so he found himself at the U.S.

AP/WORLD WIDE PHOTOS/HANS DERYK

Military Academy at West Point, playing basketball. However, Krzyzewski didn't want to be an Army officer. He wanted to be a basketball coach. After he graduated, he coached service teams for a couple of years. When he resigned from the Army, he went to Indiana University as an assistant coach to Bobby Knight. From there he went to Duke, where he has been for more than 20 years.

After Duke won the 2001 national championship, Krzyzewski said, "I thoroughly loved coaching these kids. . . . They've given me their hearts, their minds, and not only that, they've given to each other. That's the most rewarding thing about what I do."

Sources: "Mike Krzyzewski," GoDuke.com, http://www.goduke.ocsn.com/sports/m-baskbl/mtt/krzyzewski_mike00.html; accessed January 14, 2003; "Mike Krzyzewski," Hall of Famers, Basketball Hall of Fame, http://www.hoophall.com/halloffamers/Krzysewski.htm, accessed March 14, 2003; "Duke's Winning Coach Isn't Afraid of Losing," America's Best Society and Culture, CNN.com, http://www.cnn.com/specials/2001/americasbest/time/society.culture/pro.mkrzyzewski.html, accessed March 14, 2003.

If the group is formal—perhaps at work or with a political affiliation—you may be given an agenda before the group meets. Read the agenda and make sure you are prepared to discuss the subjects that will come up at the meeting. Preparation may involve thinking, reading, or researching. You should bring the agenda and any relevant information to the meeting.

Whether the group is informal or formal, you will get more out of it if you participate actively. In addition to being prepared, active participation requires that you

> ➤ pay attention. Use your listening skills to follow what's going on. In some situations, it may be appropriate to take notes.
> ➤ acknowledge what other people think and feel. Even if you disagree with them, you should not tear down others' ideas.
> ➤ be assertive. Speak up when you have something to say.
> ➤ contribute your own ideas. Realize that what you think may have value for the group.
> ➤ be courteous. Remember that groups are more productive when members cooperate with one another.

Norms for Workplace Behavior

If you had a work environment in which the manager often came late, was poorly prepared, and took phone calls during meetings, you would probably begin to question that manager's capabilities in leading the group. For a work environment to function smoothly, everyone should have the same expectations about the group norms—how employees and managers will agree to interact. In some work settings, the manager is very explicit about the behavior expected. But most often, managers simply assume that employees will adapt to acceptable group norms. Here are some norms of good workplace etiquette.

Attend at Work

Just as you expect the manager and your colleagues to be present at every work function that they can, you should plan to engage equally. Employees who engage at the workplace usually receive better evaluations than employees who skip important work events. An occasional absence due to illness or emergency may be necessary, but beyond that, absences show a lack of commitment to your employer.

Arrive on Time

Make sure you arrive on time on a daily basis. It is crucial that you arrive early or on time to meetings and functions. To be late is disruptive to everyone and is just plain unprofessional. If your schedule means you can't make it to a particular meeting on time, then make sure the facilitator of the meeting knows ahead of time and submit materials or perspectives that you would have brought to that person.

Respect Your Employer's Policies about Eating and Drinking

Some work settings tolerate food at the worksite, but others do not want any food or drink present, although this is rare. Often times, and depending on the environment, food smells are distracting, food winds up on the desk and floor, and trash accumulates.

Turn Off Cell Phones While at Meetings and Functions

We've already discussed cell phone etiquette, but in case a reminder is necessary, cell phones and pagers should be turned off during times when your attention is needed. If you are expecting an extremely important emergency call, inform the facilitator/manager beforehand. Then set the ringer to vibrate, and take the call outside of where the function is occurring.

Listen to Others during Discussions and Presentations

Be courteous and pay attention to your colleagues. At the very least, you will be helping to ensure that people pay attention to you when you speak up during discussions or give reports. Remember, you cannot be doing two things at once if one of those things is listening.

Treat Others with Respect When You Speak

The modern workplace contains many people who may have attitudes very different from yours. Whatever your private opinions are about people, respond to them with respect, even when you are disagreeing with them. Don't interrupt, don't dominate a discussion, and don't make personal comments about anyone.

Use Computers Appropriately

If you bring a laptop or handheld electronic device to a meeting or function, use it only for what is called upon in that setting. Do not surf the Web, do your on-line shopping, catch up on your e-mail, play games, or keyboard an assignment that is unrelated. Use the device for taking notes or accessing meeting-related materials on-line.

Resolve Issues with the Facilitator

If you have a disagreement with the facilitator or are upset by something you think is unfair, don't bring up the issue during the meeting/function. Instead, discuss the problem after the meeting or during a scheduled appointment.

These are just some common norms to help people get along in work setting and thus get more out of their experience.

> Either lead, follow, or get out of the way.
>
> SIGN ON BROADCAST EXECUTIVE TED TURNER'S DESK

Leading Groups

In every group there is usually someone who takes charge. The leader may be the person who has formal authority, like the highest-ranking manager at a business meeting, or the leader may be a group member who simply directs everyone. Leadership, then, is more than a title. Leadership is a set of behaviors, beliefs, and values that enables the leader to persuade others to act.

Basic Leadership Styles

Just as people have different personalities, they approach the task of leading a group in different ways. People differ in the emphasis they put on

> the task itself—getting a job done
> relationships with others—being interested primarily in people

> A leader has the vision and conviction that a dream can be achieved. He inspires the power and energy to get it done.
>
> RALPH LAUREN,
> AMERICAN DESIGNER

Democrats

Leaders who stress both task and relationships can be called democrats. They tend to derive their authority from the cooperative ideals and goals of the group. They are good at getting individuals to participate, because they are not overly concerned with maintaining their own authority or power. They are interested in motivating group members to share the responsibility for achieving the group's goals.

Taskmasters

Leaders who stress the task over the group's relationships are taskmasters. They are more concerned about getting the job done than fostering fellowship. They tend to be confident, independent, and ambitious. To get group members to do what's necessary, they try to control behavior with rewards and punishments. This type of leader assigns tasks and responsibilities to group members.

Nurturers

Leaders who put relationships over the task at hand are nurturers. They believe that people come first. They emphasize the personal development of group members. Because of this, they tend to be sympathetic, approving, and friendly. They create a secure atmosphere in which the group can operate.

Bureaucrats

Leaders who are oriented neither to the task nor to relationships are bureaucrats. They behave in a cautious, orderly, and conservative way. They prefer facts and established procedures to risk-taking behavior. Such leaders pay attention to detail and accuracy.

Situational Leadership

Which of these four basic leadership styles is best? The answer to this question is: the style that is most effective in a particular set of circumstances.

Although each of us may possess traits and values that make us tend naturally to one of the four basic styles, good leaders can adapt their styles to the situation. The ability to adapt your leadership style to different circumstances is called situational leadership.

ELEMENTS OF EXCELLENCE

After reading this chapter, you have learned

> how understanding the basics of group dynamics can help you function within and lead groups.
> what the key roles are within groups and how to understand their impact.
> how setting norms (rules) can help a group to function optimally.
> what you can do to develop your ability to lead groups effectively.

The Information Highway

Getting Up to Speed

There are many sources of information about groups on the Internet. Here are a few places to start your search:

> **http://www.has.vcu.edu/.** A professor at Virginia Commonwealth University maintains a page with links to resources on group dynamics, called "Forstyh's Research in Groups."
> **http://www.meetup.com.** A site puts together informal groups based on shared interests and sets up meetings, although there's no guarantee anyone will show up.
> **http://www.google.com/.** You can find an Internet discussion group that interests you and join in the conversation by selecting "Groups."

You can search for more resources by using the key words *group dynamics, roles and norms, conformity, classroom etiquette, work teams, leadership styles, prejudice,* and *discrimination.*

JOURNAL

Answer the following journal questions.

1. Describe the role you play in your family and the norms for your behavior. To what extent is having a role and norms useful? To what extent does it limit you?

_____

_____

_____

_____

_____

_____

_____

_____

_____

2. Have you ever felt prejudice toward someone else and been mistaken about what they were really like? Describe what happened and what changed your attitude.

_____

_____

_____

_____

_____

_____

_____

_____

_____

3. What was the least successful group you've been in? What made the group function poorly? How might its group dynamics been improved?

_____

_____

_____

_____

_____

_____

_____

_____

_____

_____

4. Describe a person who has played a great leadership role in your life. What qualities made this person an outstanding leader?

_____

_____

_____

_____

_____

_____

_____

_____

_____

_____

Chapter 10

Handling Change and Stress

Two factory workers learned that in six months their plant would shut down. Both felt extremely stressed about losing their jobs. The first, after a brief period of feeling angry and anxious, decided he would go back to school and acquire skills that would enable him to get off the factory floor and into a more promising career. The second worker tried to get factory work elsewhere, but no one was hiring. After months of job hunting, he lost the willpower to look for a job. Two years after the plant shut down, one man is on his way to a new career and the other is counted among the "permanently unemployed."

Why did one person become energized by the prospect of a layoff and another become demoralized? Many psychologists think that, like beauty, stress is in the mind of the beholder. An event in and of itself is not enough to cause stress. Rather, stress is the emo-

One person's stress is another person's sport. At the age of 70, former President George H. W. Bush jumped out of an airplane for old times' sake. When he was younger, he had been a Navy pilot during World War II.

COURTESY OF JOE JENNINGS

tional and physical reaction that results when a person has trouble coping with a situation, event, or change. In most situations, people feel stress when they interpret a situation as likely to overtax their ability to deal with it. Whether they think and feel that a situation is stressful

depends on previous experience with similar situations and their ability to cope. Thus, one person's stressful situation is another person's enjoyable challenge. To give an extreme example, most of us would feel tremendous stress if we were pushed out of an airplane with a parachute on our back. Skydivers, on the other hand, would take the jump much more calmly.

People respond to stressful situations both physically and psychologically. Physical reactions to stress include increased levels of adrenaline, which helps the body produce more energy, higher blood pressure, and faster heart rate. These responses can help us deal with stress in the short run by improving our ability to "fight or flee." But when stress continues over a long period, it can result in illness.

The psychological reactions to a stressful event are varied. In a stressful situation, most people feel that they have lost control over their lives and that life is unpredictable. Consequently, they feel helpless, anxious, and upset. These feelings can develop into anger or depression, sometimes severe enough to require treatment.

Despite the potentially serious effects of stress, it's a mistake to think that stress is a completely negative experience. Stress has positive aspects as well. Many people experience growth when they seek new experiences they are not sure they can handle. When you start a new job, choose a difficult course of study, or decide to get married, you are seeking stress, whether you are aware of it or not. But if you constantly played it safe and never tried something new or challenging, you would never reach your potential. You would stop growing. To live a successful life, you must handle the stress you seek and the stress that comes unpredictably.

Causes of Stress

As we've already seen, what causes stress for you may be a routine event or even stimulating for someone else. Nevertheless, we can make some generalizations about what causes stress for most people.

> Negative events cause more stress than positive events; for example, getting a divorce is more stressful than getting married.

> Unpredictable events are more stressful than predictable events; getting sick unexpectedly causes more stress than an annual case of hay fever.

> Uncontrollable events cause more stress than controllable events; being fired from work is more stressful than resigning.

> Uncertain events are more stressful than definite events; not knowing whether you've gotten a job causes more stress than knowing whether you've gotten it.

Events that cause stress can be roughly divided into two types: major life events, like marriage, pregnancy, moving, going back to school, losing a job, and death, and daily events, like traffic jams, being late, noisy neighbors, and misplacing your keys.

Major Life Changes

Thomas H. Holmes, a psychiatrist, and his colleagues did research on the relationship of major life changes, the amount of adjustment they require, and illness. They found that the more major changes individuals have experienced in a short time, the more likely they are to become ill.

As a result of these studies, Holmes and his colleagues came up with the Social Readjustment Rating Scale (see Table 10-1). Basically, this is a list of major life changes, each of which is assigned a rating depending on the amount of readjustment it requires. According to this scale, the death of a spouse is the most stressful event, with a rating of 100, and minor violations of the law the least stressful, with a rating of 11. Holmes found that when people experience a number of major life changes within a year, they are more likely to become ill. About half of the people with scores of 150 to 300 and 70 percent of those with scores over 300 developed an illness within a year or two.

TABLE 10–1   Social Readjustment Rating Scale

Life Event	Value	Life Event	Value
Death of spouse	100	Son or daughter leaving home	29
Divorce	73	Trouble with in-laws	29
Separation from spouse	65	Outstanding personal achievement	28
Jail term	63		
Death of close family member	63	Spouse begins or stops work	26
Personal injury or illness	63	Starting or finishing school	26
Marriage	50	Change in living conditions	25
Fired from work	47	Change in personal habits	24
Reconciliation with spouse	45	Trouble with boss	23
Retirement	45	Change in work hours or conditions	20
Change in health of family member	44	Moving	20
Pregnancy	40	Change in schools	20
Sex difficulties	39	Change in recreational habits	19
Addition to family	39	Change in social activities	18
Change of financial status	38	Change in sleeping habits	16
Death of close friend	37	Change in number of family gatherings	15
Change of career	36	Change in eating habits	15
Change in number of marital arguments	33	Vacation	13
Foreclosure of mortgage or loan	30	Christmas or major holiday	12
Change in work responsibilities	29	Minor violation of the law	11

Source: Reprinted with permission from *Journal of Psychosomatic Research,* vol. 11, p. 213, Thomas H. Holmes and Richard H. Rahe, "The Social Readjustment Rating Scale," copyright 1967, Pergamon Press plc.

Happiness and Stress

What's interesting about the results of these studies is that events normally thought of as happy can be quite stressful. Having a baby, moving to a new house, getting married, and even starting school, for example, require readjustment and cause stress. So when people experience many major life changes, even positive ones, within a short period of time, they are more likely to become sick.

> A pessimist is one who makes difficulties of his opportunities and an optimist is one who makes opportunities of his difficulties.
>
> HARRY TRUMAN,
> AMERICAN PRESIDENT

Daily Irritations

Major life events are not the only causes of stress. Dealing with a bureaucracy, traveling in rush hour, breaking a glass, fighting with your sister, misplacing your driver's license—all these minor, everyday irritations can add up to varying degrees of stress. Minor events are most stressful when we can't predict them or control them.

Some researchers think that minor irritations are actually more stressful than major life events. In their view, the effects of many major life events are actually caused by the daily hassles they create. For example, having a baby, a major event, is stressful for new parents. But it may be stressful not only because they experience intense love and joy but also because they are constantly feeding, soothing, rocking, doing laundry, and going without sleep.

Risk Takers and Risk Avoiders

Some people believe that change is the fundamental condition of life. They feel that new things are challenges rather than threats. Such people tend to be open and flexible, and they take risks when necessary. Risk takers accept that they will feel a certain amount of stress. They have positive self-belief, and they are confident in their ability to cope.

Assess Your Major Life Changes

Purpose: Review the major life events in Table 10-1. How many have happened to you in the last ten months? Write the event and its point value in the space below. Then add the point values to get a total. By doing so, you will better understand how stress is currently impacting your life.

Event   **Value**

_____   _____

_____   _____

_____   _____

_____   _____

_____   _____

_____   _____

Total Value _____
Now find your chance of becoming ill within two years:
150 or less   30 percent chance of becoming ill
151 to 299   50 percent chance of becoming ill
300 or above   80 percent chance of becoming ill

Your Own Experience
Remember that each person reacts differently to stress. You may have a high chance of becoming ill, according to the Social Readjustment Rating Scale, but you may remain healthy. Describe your own health after the events you listed above.

_____

_____

_____

_____

On the other hand, many people find change to be threatening. They are much more comfortable when life settles into a predictable routine. The thought of doing something new and different makes them very anxious. Risk avoiders feel that new situations threaten their fragile self-belief. So they use up more energy trying to maintain the status quo. Ironically, the effort to avoid risk also creates stress.

Stress-Producing Thought Patterns

People with self-confidence believe they can influence events and take control of their lives. On the other hand, people who are in the habit of thinking in negative ways believe they are unable to cope with change. Because of their negative thought patterns, they find many events stressful. Believing you are helpless means you lose the will to exert control over your life and your surroundings. The feeling of helplessness leads to stress.

Whatever It Takes

Roy P. Benavidez

COURTESY OF THE ROY P. BENAVIDEZ ESTATE

One morning in 1968, Roy Benavidez, a staff sergeant with the Army's Green Berets in Vietnam, got a radio call for help from other Special Forces soldiers. Benavidez jumped into a helicopter and flew to the scene. "When I got into that helicopter, little did I know we were going to spend six hours in hell," Benavidez told the *San Antonio Express* years later.

When the helicopter landed, Benavidez jumped out and was immediately wounded by enemy fire. He found the soldiers and dragged the wounded back to the helicopter. The pilot was killed as they tried to take off, and the helicopter crashed and burned.

Benavidez got the wounded men off the aircraft and set up a defensive perimeter. Over the next few hours, he organized return fire, called in air strikes on the enemy, tended the wounded, and retrieved classified documents. He was bayoneted, clubbed, and shot, but he survived and continued to help the others. Finally, a second helicopter arrived to take them out.

Benavidez was so spent that he couldn't walk or talk. The doctors thought he was dead until he spit at one of them to show he was still alive.

Benavidez became a soldier to improve his life. Born in South Texas, Benavidez was the son of a sharecropper and his wife, both of whom died young. He and his brother were raised by an uncle. Working as migrant laborers, the family moved around so much that Benavidez got little schooling. To get an education, improve his English, and live a better life, Benavidez joined the Army when he was 20. He decided to make a career of the Army after attending airborne school. He was injured by a land mine in Vietnam, and doctors thought he would never walk again. However, Benavidez recovered and became a Green Beret. It was during his second tour of duty in Vietnam that he carried out the rescue mission that brought him such great recognition.

For his actions in saving the lives of eight men, Benavidez was awarded the Distinguished Service Cross and the Medal of Honor, the military's highest award for valor. His fellow Texans have honored him by naming schools, a National Guard armory, and an Army Reserve center after him. In 2000, the Navy announced it would name a ship after him—a rare honor for an enlisted Army man.

Sources: "Roy Benavidez," *San Antonio Express-News,* November 29, 1998; Richard Goldstein, "Roy P. Benavidez," *New York Times,* December 4, 1998; "Ship's Name to Honor Army Hero Benavidez," *San Antonio Express-News,* September 17, 2000; "Navy Names New Roll-On/ Roll-Off Ship for U.S. Army Hero" and Medal of Honor citation at http://www.mishalov. com/Benavidez.html, accessed February 18, 2003.

Adaptability

People who feel they are helpless are vulnerable to stress, because they believe they cannot take control and influence their environment. At the other extreme are people who feel they must be in control at all times. Since this is impossible, of course, they react with stress even to the slightest changes they haven't initiated.

People who fall between these two extremes—the helpless and the controlling—are best able to deal with change and stress. They have the ability to change what they can change, adapt to what they can't change, and understand the difference between the two. Such people are hardy and resilient. When they experience stress, they respond with a positive attitude. Their ability to cope with stress enables them to bounce back to a more relaxed state fairly quickly.

> God, give us the serenity to accept what cannot be changed; give us the courage to change what should be changed; give us the wisdom to distinguish one from the other.
>
> REINHOLD NIEBUHR,
> RELIGIOUS AND
> SOCIAL THINKER

Signs of Stress

The symptoms of stress are varied, and different people experience different combinations of symptoms. Learning to recognize the many signs of stress, which include physical symptoms, mental changes, emotional changes, and behavioral changes, will help you cope with stress.

The most common physical manifestations of stress are shortness of breath, increased or irregular heart rate, chest pains, fatigue, headache, insomnia, muscle tension (especially in the neck and shoulders), abdominal cramps, and nausea. People who experience stress over a long period often get colds.

Are You Prone to Stress?

Purpose: Before stress hits you, it is vital to know what your "hot buttons" are—in other words, what things in life trigger stress for you. This exercise will help you to understand what some of these areas may be.

How well are you described in the items below? In the space provided, write the numbers 1 through 4 as follows: 1, never; 2, sometimes; 3, frequently; and 4, always.

I try to do as much as possible in the least amount of time. _____

When I play a game, I have to win in order to feel good. _____

I find it hard to ask for help with a problem. _____

I'm very critical of others. _____

I'm very ambitious. _____

I try to do more than one thing at a time. _____

I spend little time on myself. _____

I am very competitive. _____

I get involved in many projects at the same time. _____

I have a lot of deadlines at work or school. _____

I have too many responsibilities. _____

I become impatient with delays or lateness. _____

I speed up to get through yellow lights. _____

I need the respect and admiration of other people. _____

I keep track of what time it is. _____

I have too much to do and too little time to do it. _____

My friends think I'm very competitive. _____

I feel guilty if I relax and do nothing. _____

I talk very quickly. _____

I get angry easily. _____

Total _____

Over 70	You are very prone to stress.
60–69	You are moderately prone to stress.
40–59	You are somewhat prone to stress.
30–39	You occasionally feel stress.
20–29	You rarely feel stress.

Stress changes the way people think and perceive. Common changes in mental functioning include decreased concentration, increased forgetfulness, indecisiveness, confusion, and the mind racing or going blank.

People under stress can experience anxiety, nervousness, depression, anger, frustration, and fear. They may become irritable and impatient, and their tempers may grow short.

All these changes in the body and brain often manifest themselves in behavioral changes. Typical behaviors of those under stress include pacing, fidgeting, and nail biting; increased eating, smoking, and drinking; crying, yelling, swearing, and blaming; and throwing things or hitting.

TIPS

Dealing with the Cause

The most direct way of coping with stress is to eliminate its cause. For example, suppose you have a job that's causing you stress, like driving a cab in Manhattan or working as a short-order cook in a diner. The most effective way to eliminate stress in this situation is to get another job.

As you recall, too many major life events within a short period can cause great stress. Sometimes it's possible to control the number of such events. For example, suppose your mother is ill, you are getting married, and you are moving to a new apartment around the same time. To prevent stress overload, it might be wise to postpone other changes, such as getting a new job, or having a baby.

Stress Signals Checklist

Purpose: Are you suffering from stress? More than two or three of the following signs may be an indication that you should examine your life for sources of stress. Place a check mark next to any symptoms that apply to you.

Physical Signs
Shortness of breath _____
Fast or irregular heartbeat _____
Muscle tension _____
Nausea _____
Insomnia _____

Emotional Signs
Anxiety _____
Depression _____
Anger _____
Frustration _____
Fear _____

Mental Signs
Difficulty in concentrating _____
Increased forgetfulness _____
Confusion _____
Mind racing or going blank _____
Indecisiveness _____

Behavioral Signs
Pacing, fidgeting _____
Nail biting _____
Changes in eating, drinking,
    or smoking _____
Crying, yelling, or swearing _____
Throwing things or hitting _____

Coping with Stress

Lack of time and lack of money are common problems that contribute to stress. By improving your time and money management skills, you will be able to decrease the stress that shortages of time and money can cause.

Negative Thought Pattern   Positive Thought Pattern

Figure 10-1: Stress involves an event and the way you perceive the event. By changing the way you think about a stressful event, you can reduce the stress you feel.

You can also bring your problem-solving skills to bear on situations that can't be eliminated. Perhaps you need to be more assertive, improve your communication skills, or resolve a conflict in order to reduce the stress you are feeling.

Reframing Your Thoughts

You can also cope with stress by changing how you think about a stressful situation (see Figure 10-1). The meaning that an event has for us depends on the frame through which we see it. By reframing your perceptions, you can change the meaning of an event. Often people reframe an event or situation by using defense mechanisms. Withdrawing, rationalizing, displacing, fantasizing, and projecting are ways in which we try to deal with anxiety-provoking situations. These may be effective in the very short term, but they do not relieve stress in the long run.

News & Views

Drugs to Relieve Stress: A Treatment, Not a Cure

People who are suffering from anxiety and stress are sometimes prescribed antianxiety drugs by their physicians. Although these drugs can be effective in reducing anxiety, they do not reduce the causes of anxiety. They are relieving the symptoms of stress but not curing it, much as a cold tablet can relieve congestion but not cure a cold. And unlike exercise, relaxation, and rest, which can also relieve the symptoms of stress, antianxiety drugs have side effects and other risks.

The most frequently prescribed antianxiety drugs are Valium and Xanax. Both are benzodiazepines, a type of drug that relieves anxiety symptoms without causing extreme drowsiness. Benzodiazepines act by slowing down the activity of the central nervous system. This has the effect of calming people. If used properly, benzodiazepines are effective for treating a general, chronic state of anxiety. They are less effective for treating the stress associated with a specific event, like a death in the family or giving a speech.

Benzodiazepines have undesirable side effects. First, they can cause drowsiness and lack of coordination. People taking benzodiazepines should not drive or operate machinery. Second, they can interfere with thinking and cause memory loss, so taking benzodiazepines when you are studying is not a good idea. Third, benzodiazepines can multiply the effects of other drugs such as alcohol. When taken in combination with those drugs, they can cause coma or even death. Benzodiazepines can also be addictive. Patients who stop taking it can experience tremors, nausea, and hallucinations, and their anxiety returns.

So benzodiazepines, although helpful for some people, must be used with caution under the supervision of a physician. It's important not to abuse these or any other drugs, because the results of abuse can be deadly.

For some people, the physical and emotional symptoms of stress can be relieved through relaxation techniques such as meditation.

Instead of trying to escape or focusing on the fear, worry, or anxiety you are feeling about something, try to focus on something you can positively influence or control. For example, if you are feeling stress about giving a speech, instead of worrying about your performance, reframe your thoughts and focus your energy on preparing and rehearsing. In this way, you can acknowledge your nervousness without letting it take control.

Positive self-talk can be helpful in changing your approach to stressful situations. Telling yourself about a situation in positive terms encourages constructive behavior. You can increase your resiliency—your ability to cope with change and stress—by focusing on positive rather than negative thoughts.

You can also help change your thinking by taking a time-out from a stressful situation. Even something as simple as a short walk can provide a break and allow time for stress levels to diminish. After the break you will feel refreshed and have a new perspective on the problem.

Relieving Stress through Lifestyle Changes

The third basic way to cope with stress is to make lifestyle changes that can relieve the symptoms of stress. There are changes you can make to your diet, exercise regimen, and sleep patterns that will improve your ability to cope with stress.

> Decrease or cut out caffeine. Caffeine is a stimulant; it has some of the same effects on the body that stress does. Avoiding coffee, tea, caffeinated sodas, and chocolate will reduce the physical symptoms of stress.

> Eat a well-balanced diet. A healthy diet will improve the body's ability to cope with stress. Avoid junk food, which is high in sugar and fat. In addition, you can eat certain foods such as grains, fruits, and vegetables; these are thought to have a calming effect.

> Eat slowly. Try to relax and enjoy your meals rather than racing through them.

> Get enough sleep. You know how many hours of sleep you need to feel good the next day. Try to get that amount every night. Lack of sleep makes people more susceptible to stress.

> Get regular physical exercise. Aerobic exercise such as walking, jogging, or swimming has been shown to decrease stress levels. Regular physical activity or sports can decrease tension and improve your strength and ability to cope.

> Do relaxation exercises. Activities such as resting, meditation, yoga, and deep breathing help relax the body and calm the mind.

> Take a break each day. Put a few minutes aside for yourself each day as a respite from the pressures of life. Pursue interests and hobbies that are a source of pleasure and distraction. Even a short rest can leave you relaxed and better able to cope.

Seeking Social Support

Complete freedom from stress is death.

HANS SELYE, CANADIAN SCIENTIST AND STRESS RESEARCHER

If you have family or friends, you will be able to cope with stress better than people who are on their own. Your family or friends may help you with the cause of your stress. For example, if you are overwhelmed by the conflicting demands of studying and housework, someone may take over a few of your chores. They may give you information that you need to solve a problem. In some cases, they can offer emotional support, reassuring you that someone cares about you.

It's interesting to note that women feel more comfortable about asking for help than men do. In times of stress, they are more likely to turn for help to their family or friends. Men tend to try to deal with stress on their own.

ELEMENTS OF EXCELLENCE

After reading this chapter, you have learned

> ➤ what the causes of stress are and what you can do to reduce them in your life.
> ➤ how prone to stress you are and strategies you can engage in to lessen that stress.
> ➤ who your support network is and how they help you to de-stress.

The Information Highway

Getting Up to Speed

There are many stress-related resources on the Internet. Here are a few sites to get you started.

> ➤ **http://www.teachhealth.com.** A physician and his wife provide a good overview of the causes, symptoms, and control of stress. The site is available in both English and Spanish.
> ➤ **http://www.stressfree.com.** Find tips for coping with stress.

To find more information about topics covered in this chapter, you can do a search using the key words *stress, stress management, Social Readjustment Rating Scale, posttraumatic stress disorder, anxiety, depression,* and *diazepam.*

JOURNAL

Answer the following journal questions.

1. Compare your own experiences of major life events with the Social Readjustment Rating Scale on page 185. Do you put the same value on the events you experienced as the psychologists did? Do you feel they were more or less stressful than shown on the scale? Explain.

_____

_____

_____

_____

_____

_____

_____

_____

_____

2. What everyday hassles cause you stress? How can you use the coping skills described in this chapter to deal with them?

_____

_____

_____

_____

_____

_____

_____

_____

_____

3. Describe someone you know who has a resilient personality that enables him or her to recover quickly from stress. What does this person do to cope?

_____

_____

_____

_____

_____

_____

_____

_____

_____

_____

_____

4. What situation at home or on the job is causing you stress? How might you cope with the situation? What problem-solving, thinking, lifestyle, and social skills can you use to reduce the stress you are experiencing?

_____

_____

_____

_____

_____

_____

_____

_____

_____

_____

_____

Chapter 11

Managing Time

Nothing symbolizes our culture's sense of time more than the digital clock and watch. Now, instead of the circular analog dial, which has hands sweeping around in a never-ending circle, we use digital displays, which show that each second and minute slip away forever.

> If you wait, all that happens is you get older.
>
> LARRY MCMURTRY,
> AMERICAN NOVELIST

Try this simple test with a friend who has a watch that measures seconds. Sit back, relax, and close your eyes. When your friend says, "go," try to feel how long it takes for a minute to pass. If you are like most people, you'll stop the watch after about 30 seconds. Most of us have a speeded-up perception of time.

With such a view of time, we feel pressure to use time before it disappears. Time is a limited resource: If we don't use it, it's gone forever. The need to use time can lead to a great deal of stress, because in many cases, people feel that they are helpless to control it. And while it's true that we can't control the passage of time, we can do something about controlling our use of time. Using time management techniques, we can overcome some natural human tendencies like procrastinating and wasting time. We can try to make the most of the limited time we have.

COURTESY OF BENELUX PRESS/INDEX STOCK

Travelers hate losing time because of delayed flights. One reason Southwest Airlines is doing so well is that it has one of the best long-term on-time arrival rates of any airline.

The Tyranny of Time

Many of us are victims of our attitudes about time. We put things off, we complain about the lack of time, and we misuse the time we have. The purpose of time management is to help us overcome these problems.

Procrastination

Procrastination, as we all have experienced, is putting off until tomorrow what you really ought to do today. Some people have developed procrastination into such a fine art that figuring out ways to postpone doing things takes up much of their time!

What Causes Procrastination?

There are many causes of procrastination. Some people procrastinate because they are afraid to fail. When they are faced with a difficult task, the uncertainty they feel about its outcome causes great stress. Instead of going ahead, they find reasons for delaying.

Other people, who feel they don't control their lives, look for cues outside themselves that indicate they should start a task. You're familiar with the excuses of this type of procrastinator: "I'll start dieting (or whatever) on Monday," or "It's too cold (or hot or rainy) to do that." Some of these procrastinators even rely on astrology, numerology, or biorhythms to indicate the "right" time to perform a task.

PITFALLS

Some procrastinators fool themselves into thinking that the decision to perform a task is as good as actually finishing it. Such people might reason that since they decided to do their reading assignments sometime today, they'll go to the movies first. In this case, the reward comes before the accomplishment. Be aware of times where you make a decision to complete a task, and that takes the place of actually doing it!

Overcoming Procrastination

Why try to overcome procrastination? The most obvious reason, of course, is that if you can start a task on time, you are more likely to finish it on time. If you procrastinate, you'll find yourself pushing and missing deadlines or cramming for exams, situations that create stress. Another reason for overcoming procrastination is that timely performance of a task gives you more control over the task. When you start promptly, you are allowing yourself more time, more control, and therefore less stress. A third reason for overcoming procrastination is that you may actually get things done. The satisfaction you'll experience from doing something difficult is far greater than the satisfaction you'll get from postponing it indefinitely.

> Those who make the worst use of their time are the first to complain of its shortness.
>
> LA BRUYERE,
> 17TH-CENTURY
> FRENCH WRITER

If procrastination is your problem, how can you overcome it? There are several basic approaches, one or more of which may work for you.

> ➤ *Set a deadline for starting.* Some tasks take effort over time, so having a deadline for finishing is not enough. Set a time to start, and then stick to it.
> ➤ *Get yourself going with something easy.* If the task you face is tough and you can't plunge right in, start by doing something routine or easy. For example, if you have to write a difficult letter, prepare the envelope first. Then shift into the harder aspects of the task.
> ➤ *Reward yourself for progress.* If the task is large, reward yourself for accomplishing part of it. Save the biggest reward for completing it.

"Lack" of Time

Many people complain that they don't procrastinate, they just don't have enough time. They are beset by family, school, work, civic, and household responsibilities. Their spouses, children, parents, lovers, bosses, teachers, friends, and neighbors are making constant demands on their time. How can they ever get anything done?

The truth is that we all have 168 hours in each week. How we use those hours is the critical factor. When asked, most people cannot account for how their time was spent.

YOUR TURN 11-1

How Do You Spend Your Time?

Purpose: You may be surprised to find out how you actually spend your time. Use the time log on the following pages to record what you do for a week. For convenience, you can remove this worksheet from the book and carry it with you. Include all activities, even commuting, errands, watching TV, and "doing nothing."

My Time Log

Time	Monday	Tuesday	Wednesday
7:00 am			
8:00 am			
9:00 am			
10:00 am			
11:00 am			
12:00 noon			
1:00 pm			
2:00 pm			
3:00 pm			
4:00 pm			
5:00 pm			
6:00 pm			
7:00 pm			
8:00 pm			
9:00 pm			
10:00 pm			
11:00 pm			
12:00 midnight			
1:00 am			
2:00 am			
3:00 am			
4:00 am			
5:00 am			
6:00 am			

Thursday	Friday	Saturday	Sunday

How Well Do You Use Time?

Purpose: Now that you have logged your schedule and how you use your time, it is time to do some self-analysis.

Study your time log, then answer the following questions:

1. Total the number of hours you spent on each of the following activities.

Sleeping ___ Eating ___ Working ___ Classes ___ Commuting ___

Studying ___ Chores ___ Exercising/sports ___

Socializing with friends/family ___

Watching TV ___ Doing nothing ___ Other (specify) ___

2. How much time did you spend on worthwhile activities?

_____

_____

3. How much time did you waste on meaningless or trivial activities?

_____

_____

4. Which activities do you wish you had spent more time on?

_____

_____

_____

5. Which activities do you wish you had spent less time on?

_____

_____

_____

6. List any activities you meant to do but never got around to during the week you kept the time log.

_____

_____

_____

_____

_____

7. After analyzing your use of time for the week, describe how you would "redo" the week if you had the opportunity to do so.

_____

_____

_____

_____

_____

Wasted Time and Misused Time

People who believe they don't have enough time to accomplish everything they want to accomplish may be facing two problems. First, they may be wasting time. They may be dawdling over meals, taking more time than necessary to finish a task, or doing nothing.

The second problem they may be facing is that they are misusing time. They are spending too much time on unimportant matters and too little time on what's important. Their days are eaten away by the trivial, and they never have time for the significant tasks and for leisure.

> Employ thy time well, if thou meanest to gain leisure.
>
> BENJAMIN FRANKLIN, 18TH-CENTURY STATESMAN, SCIENTIST, AND WRITER

Another way to misuse time is to drift mentally and lose focus. It's important to stay in the moment and make sure your attention doesn't wander.

Getting Organized

The key to time management is being organized. This means you must keep your goals and tasks in mind and learn to plan ahead.

Remembering Your Goals

Do you remember the goals you set for yourself in Chapter 2? You set long-, intermediate-, and short-term personal, educational, professional, and community service goals for yourself. How many of these goals have you already lost sight of?

Setting goals is important, as we have learned. However, you will not reach your goals unless you learn to keep them in mind. Write them down and put them someplace where you'll see them, perhaps on your refrigerator or in your wallet.

Planning

A goal or project without a plan is a dream. Planning is a thinking process in which you devise an orderly and systematic approach to achieving an objective. Planning comes before doing. When you plan, you consider

> Work expands so as to fill the time available for its completion.
>
> PARKINSON'S LAW

> ➤ what you have to do.
> ➤ what resources—time, money, people, things, or information—you will need to do it.
> ➤ how best to break the task down into manageable steps.

You have already had some experience in creating action plans for your most important goals. No doubt you considered each goal separately and created plans for each. What happens, though, when your plan for one goal interferes with your plan for another goal?

> Time is the scarcest resource, and unless it is managed, nothing else can be managed.
>
> PETER DRUCKER, MANAGEMENT CONSULTANT

Setting Priorities

Time management would be simple if you just had one goal to reach or one task to perform. But most of us have many goals and tasks on top of the dozens of routine activities we face each day.

Part of planning is setting priorities—that is, deciding what tasks are the most important and must be done first. When you set priorities, you review everything you need to do and ask yourself:

1. What tasks must be done immediately (for example, buying your mother a birthday present when today is her birthday)?
2. What tasks are important to do soon?
3. What tasks can safely be delayed for a short period?
4. What tasks can be delayed for a week, a month, or longer?

> Getting your house in order and reducing the confusion gives you more control over your life. Personal organization somehow releases or frees you to operate more effectively.
>
> LARRY KING,
> AMERICAN TV HOST

Assign each matter you must take care of to one of these four categories. That will establish your priorities. Tasks in the first two categories have the highest priority and deserve your immediate attention.

Setting priorities helps you decide which tasks are most pressing. You will find that you may have to postpone one or more tasks to achieve the others.

There are time management tools, discussed in the next section, that can help you set up a schedule. But before you get into the specifics of your schedule, remember these tips:

> ➤ Be realistic about how long activities take. Some people routinely underestimate the time needed for a particular task. For example, if you commute to school or work during rush hour, don't allow 20 minutes when it's really a 30-minute trip with traffic.
> ➤ Some tasks have to be finished so that others may start. For example, if you have to write a paper, you will need to schedule research time before writing time.
> ➤ Remember that you have peak energy levels at certain times of day. Try to schedule difficult or important tasks at those times.
> ➤ Use what you learned about the way you actually spend your time from keeping the time log. What activities can you limit, eliminate, or combine with others? Are there any periods of time you're not using wisely?

Scheduling

Once your priorities are set, you can effectively schedule your time. First, of course, you must account for the time you spend on fixed daily activities such as sleeping, eating, personal hygiene, work, and attending class. Then you can allocate the time left over to the tasks with the highest priority.

Views of Time

How long would you wait for someone if you had arranged to meet at noon and he or she didn't show up at noon? Fifteen minutes? Half an hour? If you are like most people in industrialized cultures, you might wait half an hour at most. After that, you would go on to your next appointment or task. That's because people in industrialized nations have a linear view of time. We see time as an arrow moving forward in a straight line. On this time line, yesterday is gone forever, today is a brief moment, and tomorrow is coming up fast. We divide our days into appointments, schedules, and routines, and we do one thing at a time. We see time as a resource in short supply, so we don't want to waste it.

Not everyone shares this view of time. In rural cultures, time is seen as an endless circle. Days follow days, seasons follow seasons, and time is nature's time, not man's time. If one day is "wasted," another day will come. People in rural cultures do not understand the rigid and compulsive attitude toward time that those of us in industrialized societies have. Without the need to coordinate work in large factories or organizations, where work can be done day or night, rural people still tell time by the rhythms of nature.

An interesting contrast in two cultures' views of time can be seen from their calendars. In many countries of the West, including the United States, the years are counted from the year of Jesus' birth. The year 2003 means 2,003 years after the birth of Jesus. In this type of linear calendar, the years add up one by one. China has used this Western calendar since 1911, but the traditional way of naming the years in China is cyclical. Every year is given an animal sign according to a cycle that repeats: Rat, Ox, Tiger, Rabbit, Dragon, Snake, Horse, Sheep, Monkey, Rooster, Dog, and Boar. In this calendar, each animal sign repeats every 12 years. The animal signs are associated with horoscopes, just as the signs of the zodiac are in Western astrology. The Chinese consider the animal horoscopes fun, but they do not take them seriously. Rather, they use the animal signs to find out a person's age without asking directly. If you know that someone was born in the year of the Rat, for example, you can guess which cycle the person was born in and so deduce his or her exact age.

To Do Lists for Daily Activities

In addition to keeping a planner, making a daily To Do list can help you get things done. A To Do list, prepared each morning or the night before, lists all the tasks you want to accomplish that day. The act of creating the list helps you plan your day. Consulting the list during the day helps you remember what you need to do. And crossing an item off when you finish it will give you a sense of accomplishment.

Time Management Strategies

Dealing with the Demands of Others

When people start prioritizing and scheduling their time, sometimes they forget that they are certain to be interrupted by friends, family, and colleagues. The people you live with, work with, and socialize with have a right to some of your time and attention. Ignoring this fact will cause you a lot of stress, because your plans will constantly be falling apart and your relationships with others will suffer.

Therefore, you should plan to be interrupted. Leave what's called "response time" in your schedule: a cushion of time you can use to respond to the people around you. If you plan more time than you think you'll actually need to finish a task, you will still be able to finish it by your deadline even if you are interrupted. And you will remove a source of stress—the conflict between your plan and someone else's needs.

Learning to Say No

There are just so many hours in a day, and an effective time manager knows this. Therefore, he or she has developed the ability to say no to additional projects, responsibilities, or demands when accepting them would mean being overcommitted. You need to set priorities on the demands for your time. Developing assertiveness and the willingness to say no will help you accomplish your tasks and goals.

Using Unexpected Gifts of Time

Every once in a while, something unexpected happens and you have ten minutes or an hour with "nothing" to do. How do you respond to these gifts of time? If you are an effective time manager, you use these small bits of time to get something done.

The key to using time that you might otherwise just spend waiting is to be prepared with small tasks you can do.

ELEMENTS OF EXCELLENCE

After reading this chapter, you have learned

> what makes time so difficult to manage, and how your own procrastination impacts you.
> how to monitor and manage your time using a schedule and then analyzing how you spend it.
> key strategies for getting organized, and finding one that fits your style.
> how the competing interests of others can hold your time hostage.

Whatever It Takes

Donna Fujimoto Cole

COURTESY OF KAYE MARVINS/HOUSTON

Growing up in the small town of McAllen, Colorado, Donna Fujimoto Cole was the daughter of a farmer and a high school cafeteria worker. There was one other Asian family in town besides the Fujimotos, and Cole remembers being teased by kids in elementary school.

When she was 18, Cole left McAllen to attend a junior college in Texas. Within a year, she quit school and moved to Houston, Texas, where she married John Cole and had a daughter four years later. By that time, Cole needed a job badly to help pay off her husband's debts. During an interview for a secretarial job at a one-man chemical trading company, she answered the telephone when it rang. Her initiative landed her the job on the spot.

Over the years, Cole learned a lot about the business of buying and selling chemicals. In 1978 her employer spun off Del Ray Chemical International to take advantage of a minority set-aside program. Cole and two Hispanic partners were the minorities, owning a small stake in the business. But Cole didn't care for the financial arrangement. So in 1979, newly divorced, Cole used $5,000 of her own savings to start Cole Chemical & Distributing Company.

At first Cole ran her business out of a friend's office. Money was so tight that she didn't pay herself a salary. Her mother gave her groceries or sent her cash to keep going. Cole depended heavily on the help of her parents, friends, and day care centers to help take care of her daughter while she built up the business. Today, Cole's company has sales of about $60 million a year.

Cole attributes her success in part to hard work and in part to luck. "There were a lot of people who did business with the government who felt they had to buy from small minority business owners," she says. "They also saw somebody who was going to care about their business."

In recent years, Cole has broadened her activities beyond her business. She volunteered her time with 22 organizations until she decided she was spreading herself too thin. At that point Cole decided to focus on business-related organizations. For her work, Cole has received dozens of awards over the years; her company is one of the top 100 minority-owned businesses in the United States

"There's a need for Asian women to be able to grow and to learn to lead," says Cole. "They have so much to give back."

Source: Asian Women in Business, "The AWIB 2002 Entrepreneurial Leadership Award Winner, Donna Fujimoto Cole" http://www.awib.org/content_frames/DonnaFujimotoCole.html, accessed March 31, 2003; Janean Chun, "Take the Lead," *Entrepreneur,* June 1996, p. 46; Tuck School of Business Web site, January 26, 1998, http://www.dartmouth.edu/tuck; Houston Chemical Association, "Honorary Members, Donna Fujimoto Cole," http://www.houston chemical.org/honorary.html, accessed March 31, 2003; "100 Leading Asian American Entrepreneurs: Donna Fujimoto Cole; Chemical Distribution," *Transpacific,* no. 67 (1996), pp. 72–73.

JOURNAL

Answer the following journal questions.

1. Assess your current approach to time management. Are you a procrastinator? Are you organized? Do you meet all your deadlines? Do you use any time management tools?

_____

_____

_____

_____

_____

_____

_____

2. What activity do you consider your biggest time waster? What benefit do you get from this activity? Is it worth the amount of time you spend?

_____

_____

_____

_____

_____

_____

_____

3. How do you meet the demands of your family and friends, as well as the demands of school and work? What might make juggling these easier for you?

_____

_____

_____

_____

_____

_____

_____

_____

_____

4. How do you keep track of everything you have to do now? How can you improve your ability to plan and schedule activities?

_____

_____

_____

_____

_____

_____

_____

_____

5. What would you do if you had a day with no demands on your time?

_____

_____

_____

_____

_____

_____

_____

_____

Managing Money

What are your dreams and goals? Do you want to start your own business, take a winter vacation in Hawaii, or go to school full-time? The chances are that no matter what your goals and dreams are, you will need money to achieve them. And that's money over and above the amount you need for the basics of life—food, shelter, clothing, and so on.

For almost all of us, money, like time, is a limited resource. We earn or receive a limited amount, and with that we try to get by—often from paycheck to paycheck. But just as you must manage your time to get the most out of it, you must learn to manage money for the same reason.

This chapter covers the basics of money management. Before we begin, you will assess your attitudes toward money. Then you will see how the financial pyramid, with your values and goals at its base, provides a model of lifelong personal money management. With this as background, you will go on to track your income and expenses and prepare a monthly budget. You will review the basics of banking, savings, credit, and insurance. Finally,

AP/WIDE WORLD PHOTOS/MARIO SURIANI

Some people use their success to benefit good causes. Actress Marlo Thomas continues the work of her father, comedian Danny Thomas, who founded St. Jude Children's Research Hospital.

you will weigh the pros and cons of home ownership and learn about the importance of investing now for future expenses such as retirement.

Attitudes toward Money

Money is a resource that carries a high emotional charge for many people. Time, or lack of it, can cause anxiety and stress, but attitudes toward money are often tangled up with a person's self-belief. American culture places great importance on achieving material success. In this view, the possession of money is often equated with a person's inner worth. The more money you have, the better you are as a person. When money defines self-belief, people depend on possessions to boost their feelings of worth. And possessions, although nice, are not a solid foundation for a positive self-belief.

> Misplaced emphasis occurs ... when you think that everything is going well because your car drives so smoothly, and your new suit fits you so well, and those high-priced shoes you bought make your feet feel so good; and you begin to believe that these things, these many luxuries all around, are the really important matters of your life.
>
> MARTIN LUTHER KING JR.,
> CIVIL RIGHTS LEADER

How do you feel about money? Do you see money as making you a better person? Or do you view money as a tool, something you can use to achieve your goals, whether educational, professional, or personal?

The Financial Pyramid

Now that you have thought about your attitudes toward money, try putting these aside for a while. You'll be a better money manager if you can separate your decisions about money from your feelings. In the remainder of this chapter, we will focus on various aspects of money management. First we will look at the big picture of money management, and then we will consider some of the details that will help you make financial decisions.

The big picture of personal money management is shown by the financial pyramid (see Figure 12-1). The financial pyramid provides a visual model of the main aspects of personal finance. At the base of the financial pyramid are your values and goals. These should be the foundation of all your money decisions. The next step up is your basic living expenses—shelter, food, clothing, and so on. Before you can go on to spend money on other things, you

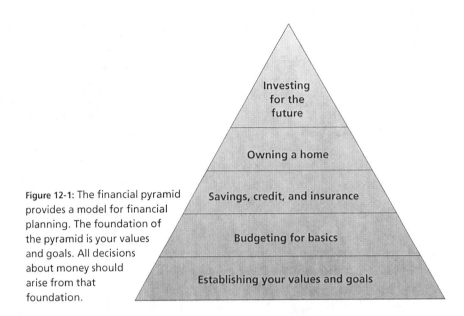

Figure 12-1: The financial pyramid provides a model for financial planning. The foundation of the pyramid is your values and goals. All decisions about money should arise from that foundation.

The pyramid contains, from top to bottom:
- Investing for the future
- Owning a home
- Savings, credit, and insurance
- Budgeting for basics
- Establishing your values and goals

must take care of your basic living costs. Once you've budgeted for the basics, you can move up a step to consider savings, credit, and insurance. When these are incorporated in your financial plan, most people are ready to move up a step to home ownership, the main investment of many families. Finally, people devote resources to long-term investing. Common goals for long-term investment are saving for their children's education and saving for retirement.

The financial pyramid helps people set priorities on using their money resources and provides a reminder of important long-term financial goals that people need to act on even when they are young. However, the financial pyramid model may not apply equally to everyone. For example, some families never own a home; others do not use credit. In addition, the model is not always sequential. Although most people consider these aspects of financial planning in the order shown, from bottom to top, this sequence does not always apply. For example, if you are living with your parents, you may not need to contribute to basic household expenses, but you may already have dealt with credit when you applied for student loans. Once families are well established, however, they are probably making personal finance decisions on each level of the pyramid—at the same time.

Budgeting for the Basics

Budgeting has important benefits. The first, of course, is that you will have a better idea of exactly where your money comes from and where it goes. But just as important, budgeting helps you focus on your goals and set priorities for achieving them. Even though your income may increase in the future, so will your financial responsibilities and your wants. This means you must think about your goals and decide what's most important to you. Budgeting forces you to make choices, plan ahead, and control your spending. But before you can budget, you must have a thorough knowledge of your income and expenses.

YOUR TURN 12-1

Review Your Values and Goals

Purpose: Now is a good time to turn back to Chapters 1 and 2 and review your values and goals. Summarize your most important values and goals below. Underline the goals that involve money.

1. Most important values

_____

_____

_____

_____

_____

2. Short-term goals

_____

_____

_____

_____

_____

3. Intermediate-term goals

_____

_____

_____

_____

_____

4. Long-term goals

_____

_____

_____

_____

_____

The Four As of Budgeting

Budgeting has four basic steps, called the four As of budgeting.

1. Accounting for income and expenses
2. Analyzing your situation
3. Allocating your income
4. Adjusting your budget

Accounting for Income and Expenses

> The use of money is all the advantage there is in having money.
>
> BENJAMIN FRANKLIN, 18TH-CENTURY STATESMAN, SCIENTIST, AND WRITER

The first step of budgeting is accounting for your income and expenses. What this means, in practice, is that you have to keep track of income and expenses for a couple of months. You keep track not only of big expenses like car payments but small expenses like renting a DVD or buying a snack. If you have a checking account or make most purchases with a credit or debit card, you will have good records of many of your expenses.

Make Up a Monthly Budget

Purpose: Use the information you gathered and analyzed to allocate your income on a monthly basis. In the space below, enter the dollar amounts you plan to spend on each of the following expenses for a period of one month. By doing so, you will better understand your money flow.

Item	Budgeted Amount
Rent or mortgage	_____
Telephone, cell phone	_____
Utilities (gas, oil, electricity, water, sewer)	_____
Cable TV/Internet access	_____
Insurance (auto, health, life, homeowners', disability, etc.)	_____
Installment loans, car payments	_____
Transportation (gas, maintenance, repairs, parking, carfare)	_____
Food (groceries and restaurant meals)	_____
Clothing	_____
Household items and repairs	_____
Gifts	_____
Medical/dental	_____
Education (tuition, books, fees)	_____
Personal (include entertainment)	_____
Emergency fund	_____
Taxes not withheld (self-employment, excise, real estate)	_____
Savings toward goals	_____
Other	_____

To track income and expenses, you can keep a notebook. Divide the notebook into two sections—a small section for income and a large section for expenses. When you get paid or receive money, enter the date, source, and amount in the income section. When you spend money jot down the date, what you bought, and how much you paid in the expenses section. Remember to enter items you purchase with a credit card. To make record keeping easier, you can divide your expenses into categories such as rent, telephone, utilities, food, clothing, transportation, medical/dental, entertainment, personal items, gifts, and so on. At the end of each month, total your income and expenses by categories. These figures will be the basis for your budget.

Analyzing Your Situation

After you've kept track of income and expenses for a couple of months, you should analyze your situation. Ask yourself some questions:

> ➤ Did your expenses exceed your income?
> ➤ Were you able to pay all your fixed expenses?
> ➤ Did a large periodic expense such as an annual insurance premium or tuition bill throw you off?
> ➤ Are you spending too much money on some types of things?
> ➤ Did you pay off all your credit card balances, or did you get by with the minimum payment?
> ➤ Were you able to save money for one of your goals (vacation, tuition, a new stereo, a car, down payment on a house, retirement, etc.)?

Your answers to these questions will point up any weaknesses in your current money situation.

Allocating Your Income

Now comes decision-making time. You've kept track of income and expenses for a couple of months and you've reviewed your spending patterns. You probably think that at this rate you'll never have money to reach your goals! But there are things you can do.

First, figure out how much you must allocate to each of your monthly fixed expenses. You must allocate money for bills you pay monthly (such as rent, electricity, and credit card payments), as well as bills you pay quarterly, semiannually, or annually (insurance premiums, tuition, excise taxes, real estate taxes, and so on). Perhaps you noticed that you were unprepared to pay that semiannual auto insurance premium or some other periodic large bill. If you set aside a certain amount of money each month, you would be ready to pay those large, occasional, but regular expenses. For example, if the cost of your auto insurance premium is $600 a year, you should be allocating $50 each month toward that expense.

After you've budgeted your fixed expenses, review your variable expenses to see where you are overspending. Here you must make judgments between what you really need and what you want. For example, are you spending a lot more than you thought on personal items and restaurant meals? If you could cut down on these expenditures, you could use the money you save to pay down your credit card balance or start saving. Try to allocate money for things that are really important to you in the long run.

Next, consider what you would do if your car broke down and needed a $300 repair. These things happen all the time, but if you haven't set aside money in an emergency fund, you'll be caught short when something unexpected happens. A minimum of two months' income is recommended for your emergency fund. That will help cover unplanned expenses such as repairs and loss of income through disability or unemployment. Remember to replenish the fund as soon as you can if you take money out of it.

Finally, consider your goals. If you want to take a vacation in Europe or buy a house, start saving now—even if you can only afford a few dollars a month. If your goal is more important to you than anything else, you might want to start the allocation process with money toward the goal. Then you'll have to reduce your other expenditures until your goal is met. Some people live frugally for years in order to meet an important financial goal, such as paying for an education, buying a house, or starting a business.

Adjusting Your Budget

A budget is not carved in stone. As you try out your budget you may find that you haven't planned realistically or you've forgotten some items altogether. Your income will change, your expenses will change, and your goals will change. For these reasons, you should plan to review your budget periodically and revise it as necessary.

Your Personal Insurance Plan

Purpose: Many people purchase insurance without fully understanding what it is they have purchased. This exercise asks that you become reacquainted with your insurance policies.

Think about your current circumstances. What kind of insurance do you need? For each of the following, indicate why you do need this form of insurance or why you don't need it.

1. Medical coverage

_____

_____

_____

_____

2. Auto insurance

_____

_____

_____

_____

3. Life insurance

_____

_____

_____

_____

4. Disability insurance

_____

_____

_____

_____

5. Renter's insurance

_____

_____

_____

6. Homeowner's insurance

_____

_____

_____

Credit

Buy now, pay later. Sounds wonderful, doesn't it? Credit is a financial arrangement that gives you the right to defer payment on merchandise or services. In essence, you are using someone else's money to pay for something. But—you must pay back what you borrowed, plus interest.

There are times when using credit is worth the price you pay. A genuine emergency like a large medical bill, a genuine necessity like a car repair, or paying tuition for a degree program are all examples of situations in which it is appropriate to borrow money. On the other hand, buying a luxury item because the credit terms look easy and borrowing when you have no prospect of being able to pay the money back are two situations in which you should not use credit.

So be careful when you are considering using credit. It's tempting—and easy—to borrow money and use credit cards. But unless you keep tight control on the amounts you borrow, the debt mounts up until you can't manage the monthly payments. In that situation your creditors can repossess the merchandise, garnishee your salary (get a portion of what you make until the loan is paid), and give negative information about your creditworthiness to a credit bureau. Credit may be attractive, but misusing it can lead to stress and financial crisis.

The Cost of Credit

Because buying something on credit costs more than paying cash, you should shop around when you're taking out a loan or applying for a credit card. Different retailers and financial institutions lend money on different terms. The total cost of credit may vary widely.

When you use credit, make sure you know the annual percentage rate (APR), which is the interest rate you will be charged per year on the amount you finance. Also make sure you know the finance charge, the total of all costs associated with the loan or credit card—interest, fees, service charges, insurance, and so on—before you sign anything. APRs and fees vary widely, so you should shop around for the best deal.

Credit Cards

Credit cards have many advantages. They relieve you of the need to carry large amounts of cash when shopping. They allow you to charge travel, entertainment, and merchandise all over the world. They make ordering merchandise by mail, phone, or on the Internet easy. And they allow you to take advantage of buying items on sale even when you don't have the cash. Of course, the flip side is that credit cards can lull you into a false sense that you have lots of money—until you get the bill. So while they have many advantages, credit cards should be used cautiously. Credit card debt is increasing steadily, especially in younger age groups. Be aware of how you use credit cards—or how credit cards use you.

News & Views

Dealing with Debt

Owing more money than you can pay back is sometimes the result of poor money management: People simply borrow too much money and charge too much to their credit cards. Sometimes debt becomes unmanageable when income drops because of events such as divorce, unemployment, or illness.

No matter what the cause, however, debt can easily grow until it is too large to pay off. In fact, more than 1.5 million Americans filed for bankruptcy in 2002 because they couldn't resolve their debt problems in any other way.

Well before people get to the bankruptcy stage, they should be aware of the warning signs that financial trouble may be getting serious. Take this test to see if any of the warning signs apply to you. Do you

> pay only monthly minimums on your credit cards?
> skip some bills to pay others?
> panic when faced with an unexpected major expense, such as a car repair?
> depend on overtime or moonlighting to pay your monthly bills?
> borrow from friends and relatives to cover your basic expenses?

If you answered yes to any of these questions, you may be headed for financial trouble.

How can you regain control of your finances? The first step is to know how much you earn, how much you spend, and how much you owe. If you can't get a handle on these three things on your own, you need help. There are organizations whose purpose is to help people having financial difficulties. For example, American Consumer Credit Counseling (http://consumercredit. com) and the National Foundation for Consumer Credit (http://www.nfcc. org) are two organizations that provide credit counseling services either free or for a small fee; the organizations are financed by lenders. Credit counselors help people work out long-term debt payment plans while learning how to budget and change their spending habits.

Source: American Bankruptcy Institute, "U.S. Bankruptcy Filings, 1980–2002," http://www. abiworld.org/stats/1980annual.html, accessed April 3, 2003; *The Consumer Reports Money Book,* Yonkers, NY: Consumer Union, 1992, p. 153; "Danger Signs of Financial Trouble," American Consumer Credit Counseling Web site, http://accc.pair.com/danger.htm, February 6, 1998; "Take a Step in the Right Direction: A Guide to Managing Your Money," National Foundation of Consumer Credit, Silver Spring, MD, 1997.

Credit Records and Your Rights

The first time you applied for a credit card or loan, you may have been refused because you had no credit record. You had no credit record, of course, because you had never been given credit. You gained credit by using one of several approaches to establish a credit record; these strategies can be used to repair damaged credit as well.

- You took out a small installment loan and asked someone with a credit record to cosign with you. The cosigner was responsible for paying if you did not.
- You borrowed money from a bank or financial institution that you had positive history with. Collateral was property—in this case, money—that you gave the lender access to as a guarantee that you would pay back the loan.
- You opened a credit card account with a low credit limit which helped you to build your credit.
- You signed up for utilities in your own name, even if you had to pay a large deposit.
- You paid your bills on time.

Credit records are maintained by companies called credit bureaus. In recent years these companies have been criticized for making errors in credit records and being slow to correct them. You have the right to see your credit record and to know who else has seen it in the previous six months. If the information is inaccurate, you can have it investigated and corrected, and copies of the corrected report will be sent to anyone who received an incorrect report. You may also add a notation to your file about any information you consider unfair. You can help prevent some errors if you always use the same form of your name on all contracts, accounts, credit cards, and other documents.

Your Credit Obligations

When you use credit, you are obliged, legally and morally, to pay back what you have borrowed. There may be times when for some reason you miss a payment or series of payments. If this happens, you should notify your creditor immediately and explain your situation. Most creditors will help you work out another payment schedule to give you time to recover. You may also draw on the services of a credit counseling organization, which can help you work out credit problems.

Insurance

Insurance protects you and your dependents against financial ruin in the event of illness, accident, theft, fire, or death and is a vital pillar of financial security. Insurance works on the principle that not everyone who buys it will actually need it. If a misfortune does occur, the insurance company pays the insured person under the terms of the insurance contract and you are not stuck with a large bill with a lack of means to cover it.

Medical Coverage

An accident or serious illness can mean paying medical bills for years if you are not insured. Yet because of the high cost of medical coverage, millions of Americans are uninsured. Most people who have medical coverage have it through their employers. In some cases the company pays the full premium, but in most cases the employee pays part or all of the cost. There are several types of medical coverage.

> *Traditional health insurance.* When the insured person sees a doctor or is hospitalized, the insurance company pays a portion of the cost, usually 80 percent. The remaining 20 percent of the cost is paid by the insured person. Traditional health insurance is usually the most expensive type of medical coverage because insured people can go to the doctor and hospital of their choice.

> *Managed care plans.* Managed care plans are similar to traditional health insurance, except that the insured person is limited in his or her choice of physicians and hospitals to those in the managed care network. Managed care coverage usually costs less than traditional health insurance.

> *HMOs.* Health maintenance organizations are associations of thousands of patients and hundreds of medical professionals. When you are sick, you visit one of the HMO's physicians. If you need a specialist, you are referred to a doctor on staff. The advantages of HMOs are their relatively low cost (although their costs are rising fast), the convenience of having a wide array of medical care in one organization, and their emphasis on preventive care. The main disadvantages are that your choice of doctors is limited and access to specialists is often tightly controlled.

> *Medicaid and Medicare.* People who are struggling to make ends meet are often eligible for Medicaid, and elderly and disabled people are usually eligible for Medicare, which are federally financed health insurance plans. In addition, some states provide free or low-cost health insurance for poor children.

Auto Insurance

Each year, thousands of people die, millions of people are injured and disabled, and billions of dollars are spent as the direct result of automobile accidents. Most states require that car owners buy liability coverage, which protects you against the claims of others in case you cause property or other damage while operating a motor vehicle.

Some states have "no fault" auto insurance. Under this type of insurance, your own insurance company pays you benefits, regardless of whose fault the accident was.

The cost of auto insurance varies widely, with young male drivers in urban areas paying the highest premiums. When you buy auto insurance, it pays to shop around and compare coverage. You can economize on the cost of a policy in several ways.

> Buy a less expensive or used car.
> Buy a car with airbags, an alarm system, or another antitheft device.
> Choose the highest deductibles on collision and comprehensive coverage that you can afford. (The deductible is the amount you pay before the insurance company starts paying. The higher the deductible, the cheaper the coverage.) A week's salary is a good rule of thumb.
> Don't buy collision or comprehensive coverage if your car is old.
> Participate in approved driver education courses to get a "good driver" discount.

Other Types of Insurance

Other types of insurance that you may need now or as your financial responsibilities increase are

> life insurance, which provides financial protection to your dependents in case of your death.
> disability insurance, which pays you a certain amount per month in the event you are injured or too sick to work.
> renter's insurance, which protects against damage or loss of personal property and liability claims.
> homeowner's insurance, which protects against property damage and liability claims.
> long-term care insurance, which provides coverage for lengthy nursing home stays.

Owning a Home

Buying a home—whether it is a house, condominium, or cooperative apartment—is the biggest investment most people make during their lifetimes.

Despite the high cost of finding, buying, and maintaining a home, most Americans still regard home ownership as part of the American dream. Before you take the plunge, it's important to consider the advantages and disadvantages of buying a home.

Advantages of Home Ownership

Home ownership has many advantages, not the least of which are the emotional advantages. For many people, owning a home is the realization of a dream. It provides them with a sense of security and control over their lives. In general, homeowners have a greater commitment to their communities than do renters.

Home ownership also has financial advantages. The biggest advantage is that paying off a mortgage (the loan you take out when you buy a home) is a way to build a nest egg for retirement. Mortgage payments are a form of forced savings because you build equity (ownership) in your home. In addition, the interest on your mortgage and the property taxes on your home are tax deductible, meaning that your income tax bill will be less. A home can be a source of cash in the future because you can borrow against it with a home equity loan. Finally, if you own the home over a long period of time and then sell it, you have a good chance of making some money on the sale.

Disadvantages of Home Ownership

Home ownership does have a down side. First, you may be in a stage of life that is full of uncertainty, such as at the beginning of a marriage or career or after a divorce, or your work may require frequent moves. In these situations, your housing needs may change rapidly, and home ownership would restrict your mobility. Not only does selling a home cost time and money but also, if buyers are scarce, you may be stuck covering the costs of the home long after you've moved out. Second, home ownership is expensive. In most cases you need to make a substantial down payment—10 percent or more of the price—to qualify for a mortgage. Then the mortgage payment is just part of the monthly cost. Owning a home means paying for property taxes, insurance, routine maintenance, and repairs. Last, owning a home is not a sure way to make money. Home prices rise and fall in the short term. In some places, prices are flat for years. On the other hand, in some major cities home prices go up fairly steadily.

Making the Decision to Buy or Rent

If you need help in making the decision to buy or rent, you can consult one of the many books or Web sites devoted to home ownership or personal finance. Many of these have worksheets or calculators that help you estimate costs and benefits. In addition, there are software packages on the market that help you with financial analysis and lead you through the decision-making process.

What Are Your Long-Term Financial Goals?

Purpose: An important key to financial success is setting realistic long-term financial goals.

Think about large expenses you are likely to have in the future. Then answer the following questions.

1. List some future events or situations for which you will need large amounts of money.

_____

_____

_____

_____

2. What have you done, if anything, to prepare for these events?

_____

_____

_____

_____

3. How can you improve your long-term financial planning?

_____

_____

_____

_____

Rosario Marín

You probably are carrying her signature in your wallet. Rosario Marín became the highest-ranking Latina in the Bush administration when she was sworn in as U.S. secretary of the treasury in 2001. Until she resigned in June 2003, her signature was printed on all the paper money issued by the United States. Marín is the first immigrant to serve as secretary of the treasury.

Born in Mexico, Marín moved to California with her family at the age of 12. She was sad about the move, because she thought she would miss her *quinceanera,* her coming of age party. Even though she spoke no English when she arrived, she graduated from high school with honors.

After high school, Marín started working at a bank to help her family's finances. She attended community college at night, earning her associate's degree in four years. Then she transferred to California State University, where she earned a bachelor's degree, also at night. By that time, she had been promoted up the ranks at the bank, and she had married.

The birth of her first son, who had Down syndrome, changed the course of her life. Before Eric was born, Marín's ambition had been to be the president of her own bank. After his birth, she became an advocate for the disabled. She took on the state of California to protect her son's interests and was appointed to Governor Pete Wilson's administration. In this capacity, she fought for laws and programs to serve the disabled. After numerous positions in the state of California, she was elected mayor of Huntington Park, a city that's 99 percent Hispanic. From there she and her husband and three children moved to Washington, D.C., so Marín could fulfill her duties as secretary of the treasury.

One of Marín's goals during her stay in Washington was to educate Americans about personal financial health. With personal bankruptcies at an all-time high, Marín wanted money management to be part of every student's education.

Source: Julia Bencomo Lobaco and Cathy Areu Jones, "Hispanas Making a Difference" http://www.hispaniconline.com/vista/febhisp.htm, accessed January 21, 2003; Ana Radelat, "Rosario Marín: A Latina Who's Right on the Money," *Hispanic,* June 2002, p. 26; "Rosario Marín '04," http://rosarioforsenate.com, accessed August 24, 2003; U.S. Department of the Treasury, "Treasurer Rosario Marín," http://www.ustreas.gov/education/history/treasurers/marin.html, accessed January 21, 2003.

Investing for the Future

In the long term, you will encounter situations in which you need a lot of money. For example, you may want to start a business or pay for your children's college educations. These are large expenses that most people cannot cover with current income. Later, during your retirement years, you will need money to supplement Social Security benefits and pension plans, if any.

Long-term financial planning is critical, but it is something that people find very difficult to do. The sooner you start to plan and invest for the future, the better off you will be. If you start young, the amounts you need to invest will be smaller because they have more time to grow. If you start late, you will have to invest large amounts each year, which may seriously interfere with your lifestyle. It is crucial to get in the habit of investing regularly, even if the amounts are small.

There are numerous ways to invest for the future:

> *Stocks.* When you buy stock, you become a part-owner of a corporation. Your profit may come from dividends paid when the company does well, or from selling the stock at a price higher than you paid. Needless to say, you may not profit but may lose instead. Still, over the long run, stocks have been the best choice for long-term increases in value.
> *Bonds.* When you buy a bond, you are lending money and will be repaid on a specific date, usually with interest payments in the meantime. Bonds usually involve less risk than stocks, but they do not have as much profit potential.

> *Mutual funds.* Mutual funds pool the money of a group of people and make investments on their behalf. There are stock mutual funds and bond mutual funds as well as funds that combine various types of investments.
> *IRAs, Keoghs, and 401(k) plans.* These are all plans for retirement savings. The money in these plans is usually invested through mutual funds or banks.
> *Education Savings Accounts.* Coverdell and other education savings accounts are designed to encourage people to save for tuition and other school expenses. The money in these accounts grows tax-free and is not taxed when withdrawn for educational expenses.

Keep in mind that all these forms of investment pose some risk. Unlike money in a savings account in a bank, the money you invest in stocks, bonds, and mutual funds is not insured by the federal government. Therefore, when you invest you must be prepared to lose money as well as to make money. Choosing the right types of investments for you means balancing risk and reward. One way to decrease risk is to diversify. That means you spread your investments in different types of stocks, bonds, and mutual funds. If one of your investments does poorly, it is likely to be balanced by another doing well.

ELEMENTS OF EXCELLENCE

After reading this chapter, you have learned

> the importance of understanding the financial pyramid and how your money management affects you.
> what basic budgeting strategies you can employ to bring finances into control.
> how credit and credit cards can spiral and negatively affect your financial stability.
> why understanding the many types and usages of insurance can improve your financial standing.
> how home ownership and investing your money can help secure your future.

Getting Up to Speed

The Internet is a gold mine of sites devoted to personal money management. Many of them are interactive, allowing you to input your personal data and come up with financial projections. For example, on some sites you can calculate how much you can afford to borrow when buying a home.

> ➤ A few of the personal finance sites are:
> **http://www.kiplinger.com**
> **http://moneycentral.msn.com**
> **http://channels.netscape.com** "Money & Business"
> ➤ **http://www.quicken.com.** To find a glossary of financial terms.
> ➤ **http://www.fastweb.com.** An excellent source of student financial aid information is the on-line database of scholarships maintained by fast-WEB (which stands for financial aid search through the web). You input your personal profile, and a search for appropriate sources of financial aid is performed for you.

In addition, you can use a search engine and the following key words to find more on topics covered in this chapter: *personal finance, personal financial planning, money management, household budgeting, savings institutions, consumer credit, credit counseling, insurance* (and specific types of insurance), *home ownership, education savings accounts,* and *retirement planning.*

JOURNAL

Answer the following journal questions.

1. Describe your family's attitudes toward money. Is money discussed openly, or is it considered a private topic? Who controls the family finances? How are decisions made? What role do you play?

_____
_____
_____
_____
_____
_____

2. What are your three most important financial goals? What are you doing to reach these goals?

_____
_____
_____
_____
_____
_____
_____
_____

3. Do you have a budget? Do you follow it? What improvements can you make in your budgeting?

_____
_____
_____
_____
_____
_____
_____
_____

4. Describe your use of banks, if any. What types of accounts do you have? What do you use them for? What savings goals do you have?

_____

_____

_____

_____

_____

_____

_____

_____

_____

_____

5. What is your attitude toward credit? How can you use credit more wisely?

_____

_____

_____

_____

_____

_____

_____

_____

_____

_____

Index

The Five O'Clock Club Series

Kate Wendleton

Celebrating 25 years as America's Premier Career Coaching and Outplacement Network for Professionals, Managers and Executives

Not your average job search guides, the Five O'Clock Club books offer advice from professional career coaches, with over 25 years experience advising and placing professionals, executives and career-changers. Kate Wendleton presents proven strategies for maximizing the interview; developing your career within your present organization; getting networking interviews with decision-makers; creating a resume; identifying the right career; and teaching methods for getting the perfect job. Numerous case studies make the content real, and easy to apply to *your* job search.

The Five O'Clock Club books give you the knowledge you need to:

- Develop your own "accomplishment statement" that you can use in your resume, cover letters, interviews, and more
- Create a winning resume that gets you in-person meetings
- Use the internet to effectively research your targets
- Secure informational meetings and networking interviews with organization decision-makers
- Gain power in the interview process
- Turn interviews into offers
- Use Kate's Four-Step Salary Negotiation Method
- Enhance your interpersonal skills to survive and thrive once you get the job

Mastering the Job Interview and Winning the Money Game
ISBN: 1-4180-1500-8

Navigating Your Career: Develop Your Plan, Manage Your Boss, Get Another Job Inside
ISBN: 1-4180-1501-6

Shortcut Your Job Search: The Best Way to Get Meetings
ISBN: 1-4180-1502-4

Packaging Yourself: The Targeted Résumé
ISBN: 1-4180-1503-2

Targeting a Great Career
ISBN: 1-4180-1504-0

Launching the Right Career
ISBN: 1-4180-1505-9

258 pp., 7 3/8" x 9 1/4", softcover

About the Author:

Kate Wendleton is a nationally syndicated careers columnist and recognized authority on career development, having appeared on *The Today Show*, CNN, CNBC, *Larry King Live*, National Public Radio, CBS, and in the *New York Times, Chicago Tribune, Wall Street Journal, Fortune, Business Week*, and other national media. She has been a career coach since 1978 when she founded The Five O' Clock Club and developed its methodology to help job hunters and career changers at all levels. This methodology is now used throughout the US and Canada where Five O' Clock Club members meet regularly. Kate is also the founder of Workforce America, a not-for-profit organization serving adult job hunters in Harlem. A former CFO of two small companies, Kate has twenty years of business experience, as well as an MBA.

www.cengage.com/delmar

To place an order please call: (800) 347-7707 or fax: (859) 647-5963
Mailing Address: Cengage Distribution Center, Attn: Order Fulfillment, 10650 Toebben Dr., Independence, KY 41051